The Basic Steps to Successful Homeschooling

by Vicki A. Brady

Vital Issues Press

Vital Issues Press
P.O. Box 53788
Lafayette, Louisiana 70505

Library of Congress Card Catalog Number 95-081583
ISBN 1-56384-113-4

Printed in the U.S.A.

Dedication

To my wonderful, exciting, supportive husband, Terry, and to my loving daughter, Emily, who knows more than most how God can work all things for good.

In memory of Mary Elizabeth Brady, whom I loved dearly.

Contents

Preface

When I first began homeschooling, I read every book that was printed about the subject. Too often, I would be reading a book that sounded pretty good only to become skeptical once I learned the author had been a professional educator who was now homeschooling or had never homeschooled to begin with. I had this idea that "it was easy for them to say" because they had such an extensive educational background. Why couldn't just a plain, old (well, not so old) mom write a how-to book?

Here it is! A homeschool how-to book written by a plain, not so old, homeschool mom.

What gives me the right to speak into your life about this subject? Over eighteen years ago, God blessed us with a beautiful baby girl, perfect in every way until she contracted a very rare disease at the ripe old age of five months and three weeks. While in the hospital in intensive care, unknown to us at the time, our daughter was medically "experimented" on. Several times during her five-month hospital stay, we were advised to make funeral arrangements.

God blessed, our daughter survived, and at age five we enrolled her in a private, Christian preschool for three- and four-year-olds. Halfway through the term, her teacher came to us and told us she was having great difficulty with our daughter's ability to learn. About the same time, we took our daughter to a speech therapist to get help for her speech difficulties, only to learn that she had more problems than just her speech. To make a long story short, after evaluations by doctors, therapists, psychologists, and teachers, it was determined that our daughter, more than likely due to the medical experiments during her hospitalization, had severe learning disabilities leaving her ineducable. What a shock! The teacher at her preschool said it would be fine to let her finish out her year in school, but that she would not be able to return the next year for kindergarten due to the complex learning disabilities, which her school was not equipped to handle. We checked into special education programs in the public school. They intended to teach her as much as she would need to know to "survive," but we were told that teaching her to read and write were out of the question.

What was a mother to do? All the dreams and visions we held for our little girl came crashing down as one of her therapists assured us that the most she could look forward to in her adult life was possibly doing some assembly work in a halfway house for the "underachiever." About the time we began to crumble beneath a load of "no hope," a remarkable thing happened.

One evening while my daughter was snuggled up on my lap, I discovered something about the worksheet she had brought home from the preschool. As usual, it was marked all wrong, but something caught my eye. One of the squares contained a picture of a crown with a choice of three letters at the bottom. The student was asked to circle the letter that represented the beginning sound. It dawned on me that I knew my little girl would have no concept as to what that picture was. I asked her about the picture, and, sure enough, she had no clue.

As she sat on my lap, I began to describe a king and a queen, and by the time I was through, she understood what a crown was. Now we looked at the picture, and, lo and behold, she had no trouble picking out the beginning sound.

I began to get just a little excited and tried the next picture and the next and the next. The same thing happened over and over. Amazing! My daughter could learn.

During this same period of time, a new family arrived at our church who was doing something rather unique and unheard of: they were homeschooling their seven children. They explained to us that when their oldest son was in the third grade, the school intended to hold him back for a year because his reading was not at grade level and they thought him to be somewhat "slow." The parents decided to pull him out of school and teach him at home. Now this was back in the seventies, when the few homeschoolers around were thought to be "fruit loops" and "looneytunes," castoffs from the hippie generation. This family, hardly from that genre, began to homeschool their son along with his brothers and sisters. This "slow" young man went on to graduate from my husband's Bible college with a bachelor's and a master's degree, all at the same time and in only three years. They suggested we consider homeschooling our daughter and offered to show us what they were doing and take time to give us any assistance we needed.

That first year our daughter was only six, legally not required to be in school and already declared ineducable by the so-called professionals, so we felt we had nothing to lose. I began using materials I already had, which were all those sheets she worked on in the preschool that were marked wrong. Slowly, we began adding other materials as we were fortunate to have a very good friend who was a special education teacher in the public school system.

She gave me ideas, books, and materials that she no longer needed and had intended to discard.

And, now for the "rest of the story." In 1994, my daughter received her high-school diploma, and I am pleased to report that she can read, write, and operate a computer better than her plain, not so old mother.

The point of the above testimony is that with God, nothing is impossible. If I can do it, you can. In the pages to follow, I will tell you about some of the things we did, mistakes we made, and materials we found in order to assist you in making your homeschooling experience the best it can possibly be.

Acknowledgments

I would like to gratefully acknowledge Samuel, Benjamin, James, Helen, Connie, and Anna, who have been extremely patient with their mommy during this project. I would also like to express heartfelt appreciation to Gail and Garry Sams, who dropped everything to read parts of the manuscript when I panicked, thinking I might be off base, and to Lance and Joanna Miller, who made me feel like supermom. Thank you, Janne Beach, for supporting me in my decision to homeschool in the first place.

Introduction

You may find this book unusual when compared to other how-to books and may be a little confused unless you understand the following:

1. This book is intended to *help you* once you have made your decision to homeschool, *not to convince you* to homeschool.

2. Because there is no need to reinvent the wheel, at the end of each chapter I provide a recommended reading list of other books that may deal in depth with what I cover generally.

3. This book is intended to network you into other books and resources that can give you specialized assistance in some areas. There has not been one homeschool book written that will meet everybody's needs, and I don't intend for this one to be the first. There are too many other good books out there that simply cannot be duplicated.

4. Just about every book and resource I write about in this book can be gotten through a Great Christian Books catalog. I didn't plan it that way, but if I could have, I would have. Great Christian Books is doing a great job of supplying homeschoolers with discounted materials. Call 1-800-755-5422 and ask them for a free catalog.

5. When I give recommendations for books and materials at the end of each chapter, you will see that some are recommended in several different chapters. That is because several of the books and products are multipurposed and needed in several areas.

6. If you have children in the public school and you want to take them out right away, begin reading this book at step 13: "The Fast Track." After you get down the track, go back and begin with step 1.

7. At the time this book went to press all phone numbers and addresses were correct. However, if you find something has changed since then, and you are unable to make contact with a resource I've listed, write to me at the Home Education Radio Network and I will do what I can to remedy that. See chapter 17 for my address and contact numbers.

Step One:

Convicted or Convinced

Let me break a cardinal rule by beginning this chapter with a negative. This book is not designed to *convince* anyone to homeschool. Why? Because I do not believe anyone should be convinced to homeschool or to go to a public school or a private school. I believe each family must be *convicted* to do whatever it is God asks them to do with their children.

When we first began homeschooling it was a novel idea and relatively unheard of in most circles. When we homeschooled the first year, we did it with the sense of "well, we've got nothing to lose." Our daughter was only six and not required to be in school because of her age and disabilities. By the second year, we found that we enjoyed so much about it that it became a preference to homeschool, yet we still had our doubts. By our third year, we were firmly convicted that homeschooling our daughter was what God wanted us to do. Since then, we have had no doubts as to what God has called us to do, although sometimes the enemy reminds us of our inadequacies.

How Do You Know If God
Has Convicted You to Homeschool?

I cannot answer that question for you; I can only tell you what God did for me. A preacher once told me, "A preference is something you 'prefer' to do, but a conviction is something you would die for." At the time he was, in a round about way, rebuking me for an immature stand I was taking on what seemed to be at the time a very important issue. The subject of women wearing pants was being hotly debated in our church, and I tend to get very passionate about something I firmly believe in. When the pastor raised the idea of a conviction being something I would die for, I was stopped cold. I can think of a few things I would be willing to die for (very few), but I had to admit that wearing a dress was not one of them.

Ask yourself, "Has God so moved in your heart that you would be willing to suffer imprisonment, even death, to be able to teach your children at home?" Of course, if we died, who would teach the children?

Suppose the government of your country (I am optimistic that this will be read in more than just the United States of America) declared tomorrow that teaching your children at home was now illegal and that continuing to do so would bring fines, prison, or even death. What would you do?

Understand, the issue here is not the locality at which our children are placed to learn; it is a question of who has been given the responsibility to raise and educate our children. God is the one who gives children to us. He holds *us* responsible for them, not the government, not the schools and not the social workers. No matter which educational institution you choose to teach your children—be it private, public or home—you are ultimately responsible. You must do as much research as you can before you make this decision because, trust me, your decision, no matter which one it is, will be challenged. It will be criticized by family, friends, the church, the community, and, in some cases, the government. The only way you will be able to stand under such pressure is to know you are standing on the Rock, that being the Lord Jesus Christ, and His will for your life.

When we first began to homeschool, we were criticized by family members who thought our daughter would not get the "professional" help she needed, by public school friends who felt Christians needed to be missionaries in the schools, by Christian school friends who felt my daughter would not be socialized well enough, and by church leaders who felt the issue of homeschooling could become divisive in the church. The only people who weren't critical of us were our unsaved family and friends who already thought we were wacko and saw this as just a "church" thing. Talk about pressure!

My counsel to you is to do your homework. Investigate homeschooling carefully and get all the counsel you can from friends, loved ones, and church leadership. Take it all before the Lord, make your decision and then stand on it.

What If God Changes His Mind?

Is it possible for God to ask you to homeschool now and perhaps do something different later? Of course! God isn't in a box, restrained and constrained by walls of human reason. Just look at Scripture. Abraham was told to offer Isaac as a sacrifice and then told not to. Joseph's family was told to go to Egypt, and then they were told to get out. The disciples were told to go out and take nothing with them then later told to go out, get a sword and as much as they could carry. We are not talking about a wishy-washy God, but rather an omnipotent, omniscient Father who knows what direction you need to take and when you need to take it.

This concept may be difficult for Christians to understand today because we are deceived by doctrines intended to mass produce cookie-cutter Christians who all dress, think, and act the same. I learned the hard way that God can and does ask us to follow Him in one direction and then perhaps in another.

"Follow Me, 101"

Years ago, while my husband was finishing up at Bible college, we attended a really neat church in Denver. We loved the people, were devoted to the pastor, and grew by leaps and bounds spiritually there. The enemy targeted this church, and soon it began to have problems. I was oblivious to the root of the problems, perhaps because I was raised in a Catholic orphanage where church leadership was never questioned. My husband began to feel uncomfortable with the direction and some of the teaching in the church, particularly in the area of authority, but not me. I didn't question church leadership and believed that whatever came from that pulpit was "gospel." We began to argue at home about things connected with the church. Anytime Terry raised questions about the teaching, I would give him "the look," shake my head, and pray for what I believed to be his lack of submission to church authority. Our church and the particular homeschool curriculum we were using at the time had subtly usurped the authority of fathers in the home. I didn't realize to what extent this had happened until something unspeakable happened on our vacation.

We loved to go camping on vacations and usually went with our pastor and his family. This particular vacation wasn't as fun as the ones in times past because there seemed to be an underlying tension in my husband toward our pastor. One day we all decided to go into town and swim at the hot springs. While everyone else headed into the pool, Terry and I were having a pretty hot discussion in the camper. Terry finally said something that for the life of me I cannot remember. All I know is that he questioned our pastor's authority and motives. I drew back and slapped him hard across the face. Terry just sat there and looked at me. He didn't say a word. He didn't have to. That slap, although Terry was on the receiving end, was a wake-up call for me. At that point I was so messed up about who my authorities were, I just sat down on the bed, confused, frightened, and ashamed.

We finished the vacation somehow, and God gently began to persuade me that I needed help. While reading the Word one day, I came across a passage in 1 Corinthians, chapter 11 that spoke of headcoverings. In verse 10 it said, "Therefore the woman ought to have a symbol of authority on her head, because of the angels." I knew right then what the Lord was asking of me. He was asking me to put on a daily reminder of who my authorities were and, just as important, who they weren't.

God used a number of things, people, counsel, and verses to convince me that wearing a headcovering was what He wanted to use to help me. I began wearing one and at the same time began to de-program from some heretical doctrine I had accepted on the subject of authorities.

I wore that headcovering for two and a half years until God told me it was time to remove it. When I first began to sense that He wanted me to remove it, I was shaken. How could God change His mind? What would people think? Did He really ever tell me to put it on in the first place? These were all hard-hitting questions that had to be answered and could never have been if God hadn't firmly established His plan and will for my life to put it on in the first place.

So, what if God tells you to homeschool now and asks you to do something different later on? Let God be

God, do what He asks of you now, and trust Him for direction tomorrow.

If Homeschooling Is So Great, Why Isn't Everyone Doing It?

The criticism we received from the Christian community was by far the worse. Sometimes when God asks us to do something different or out of the ordinary, others, especially Christians, can feel threatened or hurt. Doing something different is often equated with doing something better. I must admit, in those early years I would tell my public school friends that it wasn't a question of spirituality, but my spirit communicated otherwise. Inside, to my shame, I believed that those who kept their children in public and even private school were "spiritually retarded" and would someday arrive as I had. Nothing could be further from the truth.

Do you remember in the last chapter of John where Jesus is talking to Peter and John? Jesus gave Peter an idea of the kind of death he was going to experience. Peter saw John and said, "Lord, what about this man?" Jesus' response to him was, "If I want him to remain until I come, what is that to you? You follow Me!"

When it comes to education, there are still families God asks to remain in public and private schools. I know of several families who are really making a difference in the public schools their children attend. They are there because God has called them as He would any other missionary, and they will stay there until God calls them out. Believe me, their eyes are wide open and they know what kind of evil is there. Twenty years ago, it was the public school parents who were critical of the Christian school parents. Ten years ago, it was public and Christian school parents who were intolerant of the homeschooling parents. Today, we find homeschooling and Christian school parents condemning the public school parents. We must come to grips with the fact that God will judge the hearts and decisions of every parent, and we must concentrate on what He shows us, instead of being critical or judgmental of what He has or has not shown others.

Be convicted, not just convinced, that homeschooling is God's will for you.

Recommended Reading

If you are still not certain about whether or not you have been convicted to homeschool your children, I suggest you read one or more of the following books. Perhaps God will use them to convict you one way or the other and establish a solid faith in what He calls you to do.

1. Christopher Klicka, *The Right Choice* (Gresham, Oregon: Noble Publishing Associates, 1993).

2. Cathy Duffy, *Government Nannies* (Gresham, Oregon: Noble Publishing Assoc., 1995).

3. Julia Toto, *How To Home School (Yes, You!)* (Lafayette, Louisiana: Huntington House Publishers, 1994).

4. J. Richard Fugate, *Successful Home Schooling* (Tempe, Arizona: Aletheia Press, 1990).

5. Ray E. Ballman, *The How & Why of Home Schooling* (Wheaton, Illinois: Crossway Books, 1987).

6. Gregg Harris, *The Christian Home School* (Gresham, Oregon: Noble Publishing Associates, 1995).

Checklist

___ STEP ONE: I am not only convinced to homeschool, but I am convicted by the Holy Spirit that this is God's will for my life.

Step Two:

Organization

You might be wondering why I chose "organization" to be the next step. Why not curriculum choices or the legality issue? Let me warn you, you are about to be inundated with so many catalogs, pamphlets, and brochures you are liable to be missing under the pile for days unless you are organized.

Designate an area in your home to be your office. This spot needs to be by a phone and readily accessible. I suggest that it be in the kitchen. Choose one cabinet or cupboard to be used for school supplies such as paper, glue, stapler, etc. Later in this chapter, there is a suggested start-up list of materials that would be helpful to have on hand.

The Notebook

I have used a notebook or planner for over thirteen years and highly recommend that you get one as well. To begin with, a simple spiral notebook or three-ring binder will do. If you need to, stop reading this book and take some time to gather one together; it is that important. I have tried many notebooks through the years and have finally landed on the *Busy Woman's Daily Planner* made by Dinah Monahan and published by Heritage House. It comes with divided sections that cover nearly every area of your life: a calendar, phone log, shopping list, menu, devotions. The list goes on and on. They even have a homeschool section.

If you can keep everything together in one place such as a notebook, you will not be duplicating your work or wasting precious time trying to find something you had "once before." Regardless of the notebook you choose to use, it needs to have the following sections.

Address List

The address section is vital. I have chosen to keep two address sections in my notebook: a colorful one to handle personal numbers and addresses and a subdued one to handle all of my homeschooling related business. Enter everything in pencil as much as possible or you will end up buying stock in the "white out" corporations. When entering names of friends who homeschool, jot down a note as to which curriculum they use and the names and ages of their children for future reference. The average homeschooler uses a different curriculum every couple of years so just in case you want to try something different, you will have a contact to ask questions of before you spend your money.

Monthly Calendar

This is essential because once you are used to using a calendar, you will avoid the embarrassment of discovering that you have overbooked yourself for an engagement or a field trip. Write *everything* down in your calendar—as much as you can fit in the square.

Menu

I like having a menu and shopping list section in my notebook. When I go to the store each week, I compete with myself. Prior to my actually shopping, I make a detailed list of what I need, writing an estimated price next to the item (rounding it up to the nearest zero or five). When I put the item in my cart, I write down the actual price, again rounding it up to the nearest zero or five. My goal each week is to see how close my estimated total can come to the actual total on the register tape. So far my record guess came within two cents of the actual total. Having the list in my notebook each week allows me to compare prices from week to week and see if the string beans really are a bargain.

Lesson Planning Sheets

Notebooks generally come in the 5½-by-8½-inch size, yet lesson planning sheets are always 8½-by-11-inches or larger. To solve this problem, Dinah Monahan encouraged me to design a lesson planner sheet to fit my notebook. Finally, I can keep all of my homeschooling information together in one location.

Depending upon the notebook you choose to use, you can include sections on finances, devotions, projects, and Christmas card lists. And, don't forget you can create your own.

Filing

It will do you no good to receive all this wonderful material if you glance at it once, put it aside, and can never find it again. Plan now for your filing system.

To begin with, if you do not have a two- or four-drawer cabinet empty and readily available (and I don't know of anyone who would), consider temporarily using inexpensive crates you can pick up at most department or drug stores. Boxes work equally as well. If you use boxes, select ones that will fit a letter size file and cover them with things such as contact or wallpaper, paint, stencils, or even gift-wrapping paper. Get the children involved as they will be needing their own file box as well.

As for the files themselves, you may choose to use "third" or "fifth" cut. This system works well for both. I like to hang up a piece of "sticky" paper with the following on it.

Third Cut

A B C
D E F
G H I
J K L
M N O
P Q R
S T U
V W X
Y Z

Fifth Cut

A B C D E
F G H I J
K L M N O
P Q R S T
U V W X Y
Z

Each time you grab a blank file to fill, grab the file that corresponds to the above placement. For example, if you want to file material you have received from Great Christian Books, you would get a left cut folder using the third cut system or a second cut folder from the fifth cut system. Write Great Christian Books across the tab then file it in your box. As you create other files beginning with the letter *G*, they will be filed alphabetically in that section.

I went through high school and college not knowing about the above system, and let me tell you, you can save your child a lot of frustration in years ahead if you train them in this technique while they are young. Consider having a separate box just for filing all of the catalogs you are about to receive.

It is very important that you maintain good records from the beginning. Should you ever get into a legal battle, these records will not only provide the information officials may need, they will also give you peace of mind knowing that you have the paper chase battle licked.

Storage

I happen to love books, but the problem with this love affair is that I look at these books as my friends and have a hard time parting with any of them.

Years ago I had built up a lending library, partially as an excuse to acquire more and more of these little friends. I had boxes and boxes of books with no place to display them until my husband came up with a great idea. He bought some wooden boards with some matching wooden brackets and put them up on my dining room wall about eighteen inches below the ceiling. These shelves were high enough that little hands couldn't reach them and company couldn't see dust. They were so decorative, practical, and economical that he ended up putting these shelves in almost every room in the house. They were great for the children's room, with all those stuffed toys, breakable toys, and games. These shelves will hold school material that you use one year, cannot use for a while to come, but you need to keep for future use.

Organizational tips will be given throughout this book. However, if you feel you want to read further concerning this area, I suggest you read some of the following books. These books can be purchased or, in many cases, checked out from your local library.

Recommended Reading

1. Emily Barnes, *More Hours In My Day* (Eugene, Oregon: Harvest House Publishers, 1986).

Checklist

___ STEP ONE: I am not only convinced to homeschool, but I am convicted by the Holy Spirit that this is God's will for my life.

___ STEP TWO: I have organized and consolidated all my incoming homeschooling material into one place.

Step
Three:

Record Keeping

Documentation. To some people, it is a dirty word. To others, it is permission to be obsessive. I would like to think I am somewhere in-between. It is important that you keep good records of what you have done for reasons mentioned in the chapter on organization, as well as for your own sanity and time constraints. For many, it is not a matter of being convinced that they should keep good records as much as it is knowing *how* to keep good records.

But, I have good news! There have been so many frustrated people homeschooling before you that they have created just about anything you could ever need. Let's get right to the *what* and *how* of documentation and good record keeping.

K.I.S.S. (Keep It Simple, Sweetie!)

Record keeping does not have to be complicated or time consuming. This is where that notebook I told you about in chapter 2 becomes necessary. The key to keeping good records is in knowing who you are keeping records for.

1. The first person you are keeping records for is yourself. You need to know what your child has done in the past to be able to chart a course for the future.

2. The second person you need to keep records for is your child. Remember that if the Lord tarries and your child grows up, gets married, and has a family, they will get so much enjoyment out of his past accomplishments.

3. The third person you need to keep records for is the future college registrar of the college your child wants to enter.

4. The *last* person you need to keep records for is that government employee who might someday want to get assurances that you are indeed educating your child.

I say *last* because too many people get this concept backward. Rarely will a government official require documentation. For one thing, you have the right to privacy against unlawful search and seizure. Yet, when it comes to record keeping, too many people do it out of fear. When this happens, you end up duplicating records, wasting time, living in fear, and failing to record what you really need.

Recommended Documentation

Philosophy of Education

When you begin homeschooling, sit down and write out your philosophy of education or what it is you believe about education. In the back of the book, we have included a copy of ours from 1990. When we were first challenged in 1984 to do this, my husband and I looked at each other with these stupid looks on our faces in total confusion. We had no clue what was meant by a "philosophy of education." In simple terms, it is what you believe about the education of your children. What does the Bible have to say? Research it! We finally read a philosophy that someone else had written and got the idea. That's why we included ours for you.

A funny thing happened in New Zealand concerning these "philosophies." In New Zealand, families are required to submit a copy of their philosophy of education to the education minister upon application to homeschool. In the workshops we did throughout the country, we helped families work through this by means of a workshop book we had put together. Our philosophy of education was printed on a green sheet of paper in the back of the booklet. One day we got a phone call from someone in the minister of education's department because they were being flooded with these green sheets attached to homeschooling applications. Apparently parents would read our philosophy and say, "Hey, I agree with that!" Then they would send it in with their application. At future workshops we cautioned families to at least copy it on some other color of paper or handwrite it out for themselves. The fact is, your philosophy may be the same as ours, but it will also evolve over the years as you mature in Christ and become experienced.

Write out your philosophy of education and put it in your homeschool notebook where you can refer to it when needed.

Transcripts

Transcripts are simply a record of each course completed each year. I recommend that you make a list each year of the following:

- Courses of study
- Books and publishers
- Final grades

Do this for each subject each year. If you have any final test papers, be sure to file them in such a way that they are readily available to be viewed or reviewed as needed.

Long-Range Goals

"If you aim at nothing, you will hit it every time!" I don't know who first said that, but it is true. Everyone has goals in his life which change with time. When I was in high school, I had two goals that I can remember. The first was to write a book someday and the second was to be on "The Tonight Show" with Johnny Carson. You are reading the fulfillment of that first goal, but as for the second, it is no longer important. For one thing, Johnny retired before I could get there, and for another, Johnny's role in my life is no longer important.

What are your long-range goals for your children? Do you want them to go on a missionary apprentice trip? Become fluent in another language? Learn to serve others? Drive a car?

Sometimes our long-range plans for our children are not necessarily God's. Will *He* want them to go to college? Get married? Become a doctor?

Suppose we had no goals for our own lives or our children's. We would be like pinballs you see at the arcade, bouncing from one place to another, circumstantially driven.

There is a fine line between being circumstantially driven and living by faith. I remember when my husband was in Bible college years age. He was literally chewed out one day by a fellow student over this very issue. The "norm" was to go to Bible college for four years, get a degree, then get a pastorate or become a missionary. Well, sometimes God doesn't take us from point A to point B by the most direct path. While in college, Terry started a business, did caretaking on a ranch, served an internship, youth pastored, and a host of other things, all the while appearing to be taking several different directions from what we believed God had called us to do. Terry explained to this man that the goal had never wavered. The goal was to serve Christ with his whole heart and be totally yielded to His will. He had no way of knowing the many directions that he would take.

Write out long-range goals and keep them in your notebook. Refer to them at least once a year and make changes as necessary.

Short-Range Goals

To me, short-range goals go no more than a year at a time. These goals could be what you want your child to do, succeed in, or become in that period of time. Some areas to consider are as follows:

Academic Subjects

In mathematics, English, spelling, etc., what would you like to see your child accomplish this year? You might be saying to yourself, "I don't know. He is going into fourth grade. I want him to learn fourth-grade stuff!"

To help you plan for this area, I recommend you get some of the books listed at the end of this chapter that give you a detailed list of what your child should know at the end of each grade level. One year I homeschooled using no curriculum other than one of those books—no workbooks, textbooks, nothing!

For instance, one of the books said your child should be able to count to a hundred by the end of the first grade. Do you really need a workbook to teach that skill? I have met many families that have taught their whole lives that way.

Home Skills

Teaching home skills is as important as teaching the academics in my opinion. In our home, we call them "survival skills." Just think about what you learned in high school and how much of it you are using now. Were you taught how to sort your clothes before washing them so your underwear didn't come out pink? Did you learn how to balance a checkbook, load a dishwasher, cook and time a meal so that everything is done at the same time? Set some short-range goals for the home skills each year. These goals can include:

- Laundry
- Shopping
- Cooking
- Dishwasher
- Child care
- Lawn care
- Window washing
- Minor mechanics
- Tool recognition

Plan for your child to become proficient in one or more of these skills each year and offer them a completion certificate once they reach that goal.

Character

Setting goals for achieving godly character is probably most important of all. Evaluate your child's character and determine areas that need improvement. Does he lack responsibility, meekness, honesty?

One year after evaluating our children, we decided to zero in on the whininess of one and the screaming of another. I wrote out my lesson plans to include work on these qualities. About three months after I had written those goals I reviewed them and was amazed at the progress. One child had completely conquered the screaming and was able to begin work on something else.

There are books available to use when working on character listed later in this chapter.

Scripture Memory

On the first day of each year, we gather together as a family and discuss what goals God would have us work toward or problems He would have us work on for that year. One year we declared it to be "The Year of the Disciplined Life," where we concentrated on verses that focused on discipline. In 1995, the Lord told us it would be "The Year of Fulfillment" and gave us Scripture in Isaiah and Romans to memorize as a family.

Set some goals for Scripture you would like for your children to learn, as well as verses for the whole family. Keep these goals in your notebook, readily accessible when you make out your lesson plans.

Daily Lesson Plans

I wish I could show you the pages and pages of detailed lesson plans I kept in my early homeschooling years. What a waste of time! Lesson plans are necessary, but this is where knowing *who* you are keeping the records for is very important. Back then I kept those records out of fear that some school official would examine them and use them to take my children.

As I explained in chapter two, lesson plans were only found in 8-1/2-by-11-inch size until *The Busy Woman's Daily Planner* printed some that we designed for them. Whatever lesson plan size you use, make sure it fits in your notebook.

I like to plan my lessons for the week rather than for the day. On the lesson plan sheets themselves, I will use the blank spaces to fill in what was actually accomplished on the individual days, how many hours of instruction or seat work the child completed, and which days were "sick" days.

One way to keep track of what your child is doing daily is to pencil in at the top of each page of his school work the date he completes the work. I like to use my red pencil to write the date in at the top of the page before he does the work as a way of giving him his assignment.

Recommended Reading and Tools

1. Dr. Ruth Beechick, *An Easy Start In Arithmetic, A Home Start In Reading, A Strong Start In Language* (*Grades K-3*) (Pollock Pines, California: Arrow Press, 1986).

2. Dr. Ruth Beechick, *You Can Teach Your Child Successfully* (*Grades 4-8*) (Pollock Pines, California: Arrow Press, 1993).

3. Diane Lopez, *Teaching Children A Curriculum Guide to What Children Need to Know at Each Level Through Sixth Grade* (Weschester, Illinois: Crossway Books, 1988).

4. Dinah Monahan, *The Busy Woman's Daily Planner* (Snowflake, Arizona: Heritage House).

Checklist

____ STEP ONE: I am not only convinced to homeschool, but I am convicted by the Holy Spirit that this is God's will for my life.

____ STEP TWO: I have organized and consolidated all my incoming homeschooling material into one place.

____ STEP THREE: I have purchased or put together a notebook of some kind and have transferred all my notes, addresses, etc., into it.

Step Four:

Know Your Legal Status

In all my years in the homeschooling movement, I have never actually met one of those radical, right-wing, militant, in-your-face homeschoolers we hear so much about. I have, on the other hand, met very godly men and women who love their country dearly but are not willing to let the government usurp God's authority over their children. This subject happens to be a passion with me.

We have grown up with the idea that the government has the same attributes as God. The government is portrayed as our protector, provider, and the ultimate authority to be obeyed no matter what the cost. Let me assure you that as much as I love the United States, nothing could be further from the truth. Let us not forget that governments are comprised of people who are born with a sinful nature. Unless these men and women have accepted Jesus Christ as their Lord and Savior and have yielded themselves totally to His will, they will be inclined to sin.

There is a wise old saying, "Power corrupts and absolute power corrupts absolutely." There are those in government who do not have you or your children's best interest in mind and, unfortunately, those individuals are usually in decision-making and very powerful positions.

The majority of those individuals believe the government, not the parents, know what is best for the children. Up until recently, they never knew homeschoolers existed and could not have cared less about them.

However, that is becoming less and less true as homeschoolers are beginning to organize and become more politically active. We have suddenly become a real thorn in their side. It is for that reason I would encourage you to know and understand your rights when it comes to raising your children and deciding to homeschool them.

Is It Legal?

"I think what you are doing with your kids is wonderful, but is it legal?" If you haven't been asked that question yet, get prepared; it will come.

The fact is, homeschooling is legal in every state in the union, and in most states you can homeschool with a legal covering in several different ways. In order to know exactly what your state laws are, I suggest you call or write to your state homeschooling organization or write to the Home School Legal Defense Association. They will provide you with a free synopsis of your state's laws. For your convenience, I have provided the addresses and numbers of these organizations in an appendix at the end of this book.

Do I Need an Attorney?

You do not need an attorney to homeschool! Even if your children are already in the public school system, you have a right to take them out and homeschool them. In some states, or in some cases in some isolated school districts, school officials have tried their best to discourage homeschooling by sending Social Services to the door of homeschoolers. Let us not forget that many public school advocates abhor the thought of you homeschooling, usually for one or more of the following reasons.

1. Some honestly believe they know what is best for the child over and above the parent.

2. Some believe the homeschooled child will receive an inferior education and end up a drain on society.

3. Some believe homeschooled children will become narrow and unwilling to accept alternative cultures, religions, and lifestyles. These people are strong advocates of New Age, a one-world government, and homosexuality.

4. Some are concerned about the huge revenues lost to each school district by every student not enrolled. Remember, schools are given as much as four thousand to seven thousand dollars per student per year.

5. Some believe that anyone who would keep their children at home rather than expose them to all that the public school system could offer is an abusive parent.

For whatever reason, there are people around who could make it very rough on you because of your decision to homeschool.

Back in 1984, Michael Farris began an organization called the Home School Legal Defense Association (HSLDA). This group of attorneys banded together to protect the interests of homeschooling families. The attorneys themselves were homeschoolers so they knew firsthand of the conflicts and difficulties homeschoolers face.

For one hundred dollars per year, a family may choose to keep these attorneys on retainer should any problems arise because of their decision to homeschool. A family makes application and, should they be accepted and have a problem during the year, an attorney with HSLDA will work for them at no additional charge. Not only do these attorneys come to the aid of families in trouble, they work hard to see that homeschool friendly laws are put in place in each state, keep a close watch on new legislation coming out of Washington that could adversely affect homeschoolers, and provide you with a regular newsletter keeping you up-to-date on current homeschooling issues in each state.

The key to applying with HSLDA is to do it *before* any problem arises. Once you find yourself in a hostile legal situation, you have something similar to a "pre-existing" condition, to use medical-eese, and you would not be able to retain HSLDA's services for one hundred dollars a year.

Should you find yourself in a situation in which your rights are being violated and you are not a member of HSLDA, or should you choose not to retain HSLDA'S services, you can contact the Rutherford Institute. The Rutherford Institute, founded in 1982 by John Whitehead, is a nonprofit civil liberties legal and education organization, specializing in the defense of religious liberty, which includes the protection of the rights of homeschoolers.

In the eighties, it was not uncommon to hear about children being taken from parents simply because they were homeschooled. HSLDA and the Rutherford Institute have worked very hard and won a lot of cases, which gives you and I the freedom to educate our children today.

Do you need an attorney? Let me tell you about what happened to us, and you be the judge.

Not too many years ago, while my husband was pastoring in another state, I had a knock at the door. Terry was out of town for the day so I naturally answered the door myself. Standing there was a very nice man who presented himself as being a Social Service worker. I cannot tell you of the fear that literally crawled through my whole body. He explained that a couple of anonymous calls had come through his office reporting our children as being out of school. The implication was that my children might be being abused.

Now this was a very small town. We had just come back from New Zealand, where we held workshops all over the country for homeschooling. A few months prior, we had held a homeschooling workshop in town at a Baptist church and were scheduled to hold another homeschooling workshop in a nearby town. Everybody and anybody who knew us knew we homeschooled our children. So, who anonymously reported us as having unschooled children?

We had two of what we called "the neighbors from hell." They were elderly individuals who did not like anyone or anything in the neighborhood. The fact that we moved into the parsonage, across the street from one and next door to another, and the fact that we had five children and two dogs, were a continual source of irritation to them. I tried everything I could think of to win them over, including, but not limited to, baking them bread, giving them flowers, watering their lawn, and cutting their grass when one ended up in the hospital. Nothing worked. Nothing would appease them. Not only did we have some nasty neighbors, but a couple of the deacons in the church Terry pastored had an ax to grind.

Although we may never know just who placed the mysterious, anonymous call, all of a sudden I was face to face with my worse nightmare. The man was very pleasant as I explained to him that we homeschooled. During one of the homeschooling workshops we had held, a speaker gave out information about what to say and what not to say to social workers at your door. I was so scared I simply could not remember a thing that speaker had said. The only thing that kept going through my head was the idea that I should be completely open and honest because I had nothing to hide. I *did* remember not to let him into the house but, beyond that, nothing.

He spoke to me for what seemed to be an eternity but in fact turned out to be only thirty-five minutes. He could see through the screen door that I had alphabet charts and rock, bird, and mineral charts on the walls, clearly indicating that some educating was being done in this home. He could also see packing boxes as we were preparing to move from the parsonage. Although it is hard to remember much of what he said, I do recall him telling me that they usually ignore a single call anonymously reporting a family but when more than one comes in, they have to investigate it. This gave me a better idea as to who the callers might be.

Immediately after he left I called the children together and prayed. Then I called the number of an organization that specifically helped people who had been adversely affected by Social Services and asked them what to do. Their advice to me was to take the children and leave the county immediately. I hung up and began to gather some clothes together for the children, all the while thinking this was a nightmare and couldn't be happening to me. An hour later, this organization called me back with a list of safe homes available to me in a three-state radius. Seeing how serious and organized they were really put me at ease.

About an hour later, I left for a friend's house and waited for my husband to arrive home, find my note, and call. He was shocked when he heard all that had gone on but assured me that I had not overreacted and was right to get the children away from the house.

At this point, it is important for you to understand that our child abuse laws have gone to a dangerous extreme in attempting to protect children. You are presumed to be guilty until you can prove your innocence. Furthermore, the social workers are required by law in many states to remove your children from your home until the situation and your home are thoroughly investigated. Once your children have been removed from your home, you can count yourself fortunate if they are returned to you before eighteen months have passed, if they are returned at all.

The next day I took the children to a friend's house in another city while my husband returned to our house with some friends and family to finish the packing. Not long after he arrived, a government van arrived, presumably to pick up our children. Praise God they were not there. For the next couple of days, while my husband finished the packing, government cars and station wagons repeatedly came, parked, waited, and drove off.

As it all turned out, the Social Service worker investigated the situation and discovered that homeschooling was legal in the state; he found no signs of abuse and closed the case. Meanwhile, we moved to another state and dealt with nightmares for the next eight months.

The experience we went through could have destroyed our family. It took us a full year to recover from the fear and the realization of what could have happened had we not left our home when we were advised to leave. The thing that helped us get over the fear, besides the ministering work of the Holy Spirit, was information. I began to investigate my rights as a parent, as a homeschooler, and as a citizen of the United States. I was shocked to discover how badly our rights had been abused and whittled away. I read book after book about what the Social Service industry is all about, and I armed myself with information. The more I learned, the less fear I had. At the bottom of this chapter I give you a list of books that I believe are essential for you to secure and read.

So, do you need a lawyer? Had I been a member of the Home School Legal Defense Association, the above might not have happened. Once that social worker showed up at the door, I could have dialed HSLDA's number and let my attorney intervene. To date, no family enrolled with HSLDA has ever lost their children. Had I known about the Rutherford Institute, perhaps I could have called them and had them speak to the social worker on my behalf as well.

Thousands of other innocent families have gone through what I did. In situations like these, it is better to overreact and get the children into a safe place than to underreact and possibly lose them forever. I urge you again to read the following books.

Recommended Reading

1. Christopher Klicka, *The Right Choice* (Gresham, Oregon: Noble Publishing Associates, 1993).

2. Brenda Scott, *Out of Control, Who's Watching Our Child Protection Agencies?* (Lafayette, Louisiana: Huntington House Publishers, 1994).

3. John W. Whitehead, *Home Education, Rights and Reasons* (Wheaton, Illinois: Crossway Books, 1993).

Checklist

___ STEP ONE: I am not only convinced to homeschool, but I am convicted by the Holy Spirit that this is God's will for my life.

___ STEP TWO: I have organized and consolidated all my incoming homeschooling material into one place.

___ STEP THREE: I have purchased or put together a notebook of some kind and have transferred all my notes, addresses, etc., into it.

___ STEP FOUR: I have secured a copy of my state laws and know fully what my legal right to homeschool is.

Step Five:

Know Your Learning Style

Whole books have been written about this subject, and I am not planning to duplicate them. Part of the mystery in curriculum selection rests in the subject of learning styles. The reason it is important for you to know your learning style, as well as your child's, is because educational material is designed to target one or the other. If you and your children are predominantly auditory learners, you are not going to want to get a visual program. If you haven't determined your learning style already, you are about to—and I think you are going to enjoy this part!

The Three Basic Learning Styles:
Auditory, Visual, and Kinesthetic

God put us together in a very special way. Think of babies and how they learn. They look at everything, listen to every sound, and touch anything within their reach. We continue along those same lines as we grow, but it seems to follow that one of those three ways we learn seems to work better than the others. Why? I don't know. All the experts have their theories. I like to believe God meant what He said in Psalm 139 when He said, "In your mother's womb I formed you." Don't you suppose in His wisdom He determined the learning style that would be best for you?

I remember the first time I read some material on learning styles and the unbelievable impact it had on me and my homeschooling. I am predominantly a visual learner, so I like to see what I am supposed to do. I just assumed everybody could figure out what needed figuring out just by reading what was written. Then I gave birth to an auditory son!

When you understand what your learning style is, you will be a more effective teacher and be able to choose curriculum that you connect well with. As you understand your children's learning styles, you will be able to select curriculum that fits them like a glove. And finally, when one of your children is having trouble grasping a particular concept, you can creatively find ways to utilize all three learning styles to get the message across.

The Auditory Learner

I start with the auditory learner because they are the easiest to recognize. Do you remember kids in high school or college that showed up for class, rarely took notes and yet they "aced" every test? Chances are they were auditory learners.

The auditory learner likes to talk a lot!! As babies they are babblers and are usually speaking sentences long before they are two. They have been known to talk to themselves, carry a tune, and keep the beat to music; they tend to read out loud. They will follow oral instructions much easier than written and have the amazing ability to hear every word you say even when they can't see you. They also do better with verbal introductions as opposed to name tags when meeting someone for the first time.

Auditory learners would rather be read to than read themselves and may tend to grumble when you turn the radio off while they are doing seat work. Auditory learners seem to have a head start when it comes to learning music and will tend to drive you crazy because they tap out rhythms on all solid matter! Auditory learners are great to teach because they hang on every word you say. Use that gift as a time saver when it comes to taking tests and quiz them orally a lot in the early grades. Good materials for auditory learners are cassette tapes, CD Rom, and reading aloud (get the visual learner to read aloud to the auditory!).

The Visual Learner

I can relate to the visual learner. They love to work puzzles and do word games. They are the first to notice when you didn't put on make-up in the morning because they are able to see details in art work that others cannot. They tend to be easily distracted by new sights and do not like music playing while they are studying. They generally remember where they put things because they can visualize it. Chances are those bookworms in high school and college were visual learners. The visual learner likes lists he can read and charts he can see. Some of the things that work well with my visual learners are, flash cards, puzzles and matching games.

The Kinesthetic Learner

The kinesthetic learner is the one who needs to touch or feel everything. They have a hard time sitting still and always seem to be grabbing at things. They are very animated when they speak and also tend to have great balance. They enjoy taking things apart and seem to have a great aptitude for anything mechanical. These guys do well when they are touching and feeling their school work more so than listening to a lecture or reading an assignment. You can tell a kinesthetic learner by the way he or she folds papers or bends paper clips while they are on the phone.

The kinesthetic learner needs to have hands-on projects such as molding, sculpting, or building. They need to learn to type early and will generally prefer that to handwriting. Be forewarned, kinesthetic learners do not do well with visual material all day long. Some suggestions for the kinesthetic learner are outdoor projects and nature walks, model kits, Legos and erector sets, and textured or sandpaper letters.

It is important to note that most little boys are strongly kinesthetic, even if they have a bent toward auditory or visual learning.

Beware of the Box!

Years ago I read a book on personality types that confirmed sanguine tendencies. I read all about the characteristics, good and bad, that a sanguine displays and made one terrible mistake. I began to justify some negative qualities and dismiss them with a casual, "Oh well, that's what comes with being a sanguine." That was a big mistake.

Little boys who complain about having to read books cannot justify not doing so because they may be kinesthetic learners. And, little girls cannot get away with not listening to what you have to say based on the fact that they are visual learners and would rather read a book!

I have some pretty sharp children who have heard me speak on the subject of learning styles before, and I have had to deal with them in this area. We do not want to focus in too heavily on learning areas and allow the children to be put in a "box." On the contrary, we want to look for a curriculum that uses all the senses and expands their learning gates, instead of narrowing them. Understanding learning styles is a tool to help communicate truth and academics to the children—not a way to excuse unwanted pressure to complete an assignment.

Want to Learn More?

To learn more about learning styles and how they impact education, I recommend you read one or more of the following books.

Recommended Reading

1. Cynthia Ulrich Tobias, *The Way They Learn* (Colorado Springs, Colorado: Focus on the Family, 1995).

2. Mary Pride, *Schoolproof* (Wheaton, Illinois: Crossway Books, 1989).

Checklist

___ STEP ONE: I am not only convinced to homeschool, but I am convicted by the Holy Spirit that this is God's will for my life.

___ STEP TWO: I have organized and consolidated all my incoming homeschooling material into one place.

___ STEP THREE: I have purchased or put together a notebook of some kind and have transferred all my notes, addresses, etc., into it.

___ STEP FOUR: I have secured a copy of my state laws and know fully what my legal right to homeschool is.

___ STEP FIVE: I have evaluated my learning style and that of my children and have a pretty good handle on how we assimilate information.

Step
Six:

Educational Approaches

In all the books, magazines, and materials I have read I have seen what I believe to be two basic approaches to homeschooling. I have narrowed these down to (1) the traditional, and (2) the relaxed. Some people may think I have oversimplified this subject because I am too simple-minded to recognize the deeper issues—and that very well could be! At the end of this chapter, I will give you a whole list of books that deal with this issue for you to read for yourself and make your own determination.

Understanding these two approaches to education is *critical* when it comes to selecting curriculum. More families have become discouraged and frustrated or have given up on homeschooling altogether just because they lacked understanding in this one area than for any other reason, I believe.

Is one approach better than the other? I used to think the answer to that was yes, and there are fine people on both sides of the question who would hotly debate their point of view. If God intended for us to all be the same, think the same, and act the same, the answer would be yes. If we all came from the same social, economic, racial, and educational background, the answer would be yes. The fact is, we are all different, and those differences are going to influence the choices we make in this area. The best results I have seen in homeschooling families have come from a combination of both approaches, with usually one approach or the other dominating. So, just what are these mysterious approaches to education?

The Traditional Approach

This approach is just as its name implies. It is what we have all grown up with. We began kindergarten at age five and advanced every year one grade level for the next twelve years, attending classes on average six hours a day, five days a week, nine months out of the year.

For most of us, this approach is safe because it is so familiar. Not only that, the majority of homeschooling curricula are written to accommodate this approach. Let us not forget, education is big business not just in the secular world but in the Christian world as well. From a business point of view, there is more money to be made from a traditional point of view than from a more relaxed one because the traditional view uses more books. Some godly men and women, all much more educated than I, have written volumes on the benefits of a highly structured educational setting.

I know of a family with ten children who began homeschooling over twenty years ago. They adopted traditional methods, and as a result, all ten children typically graduated from high school by age eleven, received their bachelor's degree by age fifteen and their master's by age sixteen. Twenty years ago, they had no how-to books, so they just did what was comfortable and made sense to them, what was most familiar and what fit their personalities and lifestyle.

They spent only three-and-a-half hours a day in school, but they went year round, taking breaks for holidays and special occasions. They used a very traditional curriculum that has been known as one of the best and hardest in the country. For those of you swallowing hard about now or thinking of all the possibilities success like this could offer, I have included the book *No Regrets*, which was written by the eldest daughter of this family, in the recommended reading list at the end of this chapter.

Let's take an in-depth look at the components of the traditional approach to education as it relates to homeschooling.

Age

Ages of children play a significant role in this approach. Children are classified by age and expected to perform within established boundaries. For instance, a six-year-old would be expected to work on first grade material; a seven-year-old, second grade, etc.

Time

Seat-work time makes up a substantial amount of the school hours, giving the student a lot of review and plenty of busy work but not as much time for hands-on projects.

Discipline

The child tends to be more disciplined with this approach because of the rigid schedule that must be kept.

Testing

Academic achievement is easily measured by tests built into the curriculum or provided by the publisher.

Materials

Most textbooks and paces printed are specifically designed with the traditional approach in mind.

Performance

Girls seem to do much better than boys with this approach, particularly in the early years. By the time the students are in the ninth through twelfth grade, this approach works very well for both boys and girls.

Parental Involvement

This approach is easy for parents to plan and gives the parents confidence that what they are doing is accepted in most educational circles. Most of the curricula that falls into this category is increasingly self-directed as the child matures, requiring a lot less interaction with the parent.

For years and years, this was the only approved approach to education and homeschooling around, and then came Dr. Raymond Moore.

The Relaxed Approach

Dr. Raymond Moore, sometimes called the father of the modern homeschooling movement, pioneered the way for a more relaxed educational process in the home. His many books detail the success and achievement of thousands of families who have dared to try this new approach. The increased production of unit studies are a direct result of this method and proof of its educational excellence.

One cannot discuss a more relaxed approach to education without mentioning Charlotte Mason. Charlotte was responsible for changing the whole approach to education in Great Britain over one hundred years ago. Many families are using her methods today with great success.

It needs to be said that even though this approach is relaxed, it is by no means unstructured. I recommend that you read the books in the recommended reading list and give some serious consideration to this approach to education.

The relaxed approach is comprised of the following components.

Age

All ages can be working on the same concept, project, idea, or material at the same time. Less attention is given to what a child should know at any particular age. Teaching is directed at interest rather than age.

Time

Much of the time is spent looking, touching, exploring, and reading, with less time devoted to actual seat work.

Discipline

Children tend to be less inclined to develop work/study habits for seat time during the early years, but they do well in the later years. Children using this approach have a greater affinity to stick with a hands-on project and see it through because it is something they have chosen out of interest.

Testing

Measurable progress may be difficult to test with this approach because the student may learn a concept in third grade normally not taught or tested until seventh, or they may not learn something until seventh that is tested in the third or fourth grade.

Material

Although textbooks and paces can be used, the unit studies are especially designed for a more relaxed, untraditional approach. This is where most parents make the mistake of buying the wrong material for the wrong approach.

Performance

Girls and especially boys do very well with this in the early grades. This approach teaches to their interests and helps develop a love for learning at the youngest level.

Parental Involvement

This approach requires much more parental planning and involvement. The extra time spent can actually be saved when you consider you are involved with all the children at the same time.

In Summary . . .

As you can see, both approaches have their merit. As for our family, we have been happy applying both. As these approaches pertain to curriculum, it is critical to understand that if you lean toward a pretty disciplined, routine school schedule, using a unit study may not be the best for you. Conversely, if you want a more relaxed and experimental classroom, a rigid, traditional program might be very frustrating.

Here is where I recommend that you use the Curriculum Evaluation Sheet in the back of this book. Along with that, begin to read Mary Pride's *The Big Book of Home Learning*. In Mary Pride's books, each curriculum has been very carefully scrutinized and evaluated. The more you read about the approach of the curriculum, the better decision you will be able to make.

Now would be a fine time to talk to all those homeschooling parents you have met over the years and ask them specific questions about their program and curriculum. Another good idea is to think about all the families that you know who homeschool. What are their children like? What are their attitudes? Academic progress? Overall abilities? Think about all the homeschooling children you know personally and ask yourself which ones stand out in a positive way and which ones appear to have a solid spiritual walk. Think about which of those families you would enjoy having over for a barbecue. Once you answer these questions, you will have a direction to follow up on.

Years ago, we were attending a very good church in Denver when this question was put before us. A debate was going on in the church over a particular curriculum some families, including ours, were using. A friend in the church simply suggested we think about the neatest families we knew in the church and find out what approach and curriculum they used. We did this and discovered not one of these families was using the curriculum in question.

In the next chapter we deal specifically with curriculum, but remember: choosing the curriculum you want depends upon the learning styles in your family and the educational approach you have decided to take.

Recommended Reading

1. Mary Pride, *The Big Book of Home Learning, Volume I* (Wheaton, Illinois: Crossway Books, 1990).

2. Susan Schaeffer Macaulay, *For the Children's Sake* (Wheaton, Illinois: Crossway Books, 1984).

3. Dr. Raymond Moore, *The Successful Homeschool Family Handbook* (Nashville, Tennessee: Thomas Nelson Publishers, 1994).

4. Dr. Ruth Beechick, *The Three R's Series* (Pollock Pines, California: Arrow Press, 1986).

5. Dr. Ruth Beechick, *You Can Teach Your Child Successfully (Grades 4-8)* (Pollock Pines, California: Arrow Press, 1993).

6. Diane Lopez, *Teaching Children: A Curriculum Guide to What Children Need to Know at Each Level Through Grade Six* (Westchester, Illinois: Crossway Books, 1988).

7. Karen Andreola, *Parents Review Magazine, The Charlotte Mason Approach* (Charlotte Mason Research and Supply, P.O. Box 936, Elkton, Maryland, 21922-0936).

8. Alexandra Swan, *No Regrets* (Alexandra Swan, HC12, Box 7A, 116 Hwy 28, Anthony, NM 88021).

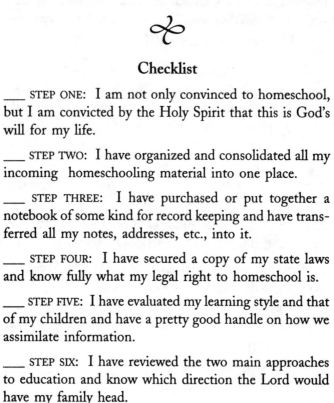

Checklist

____ STEP ONE: I am not only convinced to homeschool, but I am convicted by the Holy Spirit that this is God's will for my life.

____ STEP TWO: I have organized and consolidated all my incoming homeschooling material into one place.

____ STEP THREE: I have purchased or put together a notebook of some kind for record keeping and have transferred all my notes, addresses, etc., into it.

____ STEP FOUR: I have secured a copy of my state laws and know fully what my legal right to homeschool is.

____ STEP FIVE: I have evaluated my learning style and that of my children and have a pretty good handle on how we assimilate information.

____ STEP SIX: I have reviewed the two main approaches to education and know which direction the Lord would have my family head.

Step Seven:

Curriculum Choices

Choosing the Right Material

When I was a little girl, my uncle had an 8-mm movie camera that he dug out every now and then to film the family in action, usually at the most unflattering moments. The movies were funny then; they are hilarious now! When my husband and I got married, we made up a wish list of those things we would someday like to own and included a movie camera somewhere near the bottom. After our daughter arrived, the desire for a camera became consuming. Our reticular activating systems kicked into high gear, and we were practically obsessed. But, we held back. We knew some day they would make a movie camera that had sound and wouldn't require you to develop rolls and rolls of film. We were determined to hold out.

Every year some new, creative feature was brought out on movie cameras, and every year we said we would wait just one more year, hoping for the latest model. Not too much later the video camcorders were introduced. Finally, there was a camera that had sound and no developing headaches. Did we buy one? No! We were still waiting for the new, improved model that would surely be the best. We had this nagging fear of investing in something that would be obsolete before it was out of the box. We had this same approach and problem when we went shopping for a computer.

Well, we finally got the video camera, thirteen years after it appeared on that first wish list. We probably would still be holding out if it had not been for a vacation, my birthday, and a great sale all happening in the same week.

Parents approach curriculum in much the same way. We put off investing in this reading program or that science curriculum because we are afraid it is not the best. What if there is something better coming out next year, or suppose we move to another state and it doesn't meet that state's standards?

Let's face it. Anyone who has ever entered a curriculum fair where thousands of books are on display, each one promising to make your child a godly Einstein, has suffered acute confusion regarding curriculum selection. I must admit, I myself have spent perhaps hundreds of dollars on curricula that turned out to be a total waste.

So, how do you select the right curriculum? Is it possible to hit the mark every time?

I have good news! I am about to take the mystery out of curriculum fairs and save you hours of heart palpitations and hundreds of dollars to boot.

Door Number One, Door Number Two, or Door Number Three?

Are you old enough to remember the game show "Let's Make A Deal" with Monte Hall? Well, curriculum fairs can seem a lot like that game show if you don't know what you are doing or don't know what you're looking for. I think it was, in many ways, much simpler years ago when we didn't have so many choices. Think about the pioneers of the 1800s who usually had only two outfits to their name. One was for every day, the other for Sundays or special occasions, such as marrying or burying. Just think of all the time we spend picking out the right thing to wear every day. Sometimes, we have to make those decisions several times a day.

Curriculum choices can be equally time-consuming and expensive if you are not careful. To begin with, I believe curricula can all be categorized behind one of three "doors."

Door Number One: The Textbook Approach

This curriculum approach is perhaps the most popular, but not necessarily because it is the best. It is the one that most of us grew up with. In traditional school settings, you would receive four to six textbooks for the year, maybe one for math, reading, history, social studies, or science. Each textbook would usually have a workbook to go along with it, and the process was a real no brainer. You went from cover to cover in one year, and, by odd coincidence, by the time you finished the textbook, the school year was over. Do you suppose the books were designed that way?

Among homeschooling circles, some of the more well known textbook producers are Bob Jones University Press and Abeka. These companies and others like them have worked hard to put together the best textbooks money can buy. To get a fairly complete list of homeschool textbook providers, I refer you to Mary Pride's four-book series, *The Big Book of Home Learning.* As we discussed in a previous chapter, the textbook approach to education does not go over well with the more relaxed methods of teaching, so you must weigh carefully the pros and cons.

Pros

Confidence: For families wanting a structured curriculum carefully laid out, the textbook approach is just the ticket. Textbooks are teacher friendly, and some come with such detailed lesson plans for the parent that you can administer the course with complete confidence that all the bases are covered.

Spiral: Textbooks are usually spiral by design, which means they give you a little information then spend time reviewing what you just learned before you get just a bit more new information, then review, etc. You can rest assured that the subject matter will be thoroughly covered.

Familiar: Textbooks are great for the beginning homeschooler because they are familiar. Most of us grew up with this approach, so we have had some experience with it.

Visual: Textbooks are great for visual learners and self-starters and excellent for the older student studying biology or chemistry.

Grading: Textbooks are easily administered and easily graded.

Cons

Boring: Textbooks can be boring! Come on now, you remember how boring some of those subjects were in school. Textbooks appeal to visual learners and can be frustrating to the kinesthetic or auditory child. On the other hand, they can also help stretch those same learners.

Doctrine: Some Christian textbook producers have become more interested in pushing a particular doctrine than with sound educational content. I believe a good secular book is better than a lousy Christian book. Carefully inspect the doctrine of any textbook.

Expensive: Textbooks can be very expensive. If you have a number of children, you can pass them down, so that is helpful. Sometimes you can recover part of the cost by selling them to another homeschooler.

Education has become big business, and once you buy into a line of textbooks, you may feel trapped into staying with that company lest your child miss something in the transition to another system. Be careful not to be lulled into that false sense of security.

Door Number Two: The Pace System

About eighteen years ago while living in California, a friend of ours told us about this great, new approach to education the local Christian school was using. They were using paces in the classroom. Paces are small versions of the larger textbook. Instead of buying one textbook per subject per student per year, you end up buying ten or more individual booklets, known as paces, per student per year. Paces are even more spiral than textbooks and cover new material extremely well. The more popular examples of pace systems are Accelerated Christian Education (ACE), Alpha Omega, and Christian Light.

Pros

Visual: Paces work well for the visual learner and are great for students who need short-term reinforcement. With paces, they do not have to wait a whole year to finish a textbook and can feel successful after completing each pace.

Disciplined: Paces are terrific for self-starters or students who are extremely disciplined. High-school-age students like paces because they can complete all the work in a relatively short period of time and then get on with a part-time job, apprenticeship opportunity, or some other project.

Self-directed: Parents like paces because they are very self-directed. They can give the assignments and get on with baking cookies. There is not as much supervision required with paces, especially in the upper grades.

Testing: Some paces have built-in achievement tests that are easily documented for graduation requirements. There are also companies and ministries that will grade all the paces for you, keep records, and provide a nationally recognized diploma.

Cons

Boring: Paces can be boring! Whenever I have asked students why they stopped using the paces, the answer was the same: too boring. That's not to say there are not many, many students using them quite successfully. I have wondered if the bored students were strongly auditory or kinesthetic or just a little bit lazy. Using a pace system requires a great deal of discipline on the part of the student.

Visual: Auditory and kinesthetic learners tend to have trouble with paces, especially in the early grades. No matter what kind of learner you have, I recommend you integrate a pace system with some hands-on project.

Expensive: Paces can be expensive because they are not reusable, so I recommend that large families or families on a tight budget think twice about using them.

Door Number Three: Unit Studies

A unit study is dearly loved by the untraditional thinkers and families. A unit study is when you take one topic, subject, or word and build an entire curriculum around it. For instance, one day we checked out a craft book at the library that showed you how to make replicas of log cabins by rolling pieces of newspaper around pencils and then gluing them together to form a house. One of the children asked questions about who lived in log cabins and where were they made, which led us to check out another book on famous frontiersmen. To make a long story short, we spent an entire quarter with just these two books and one topic, yet we covered every discipline we needed. We learned math concepts as we measured out the logs for the cabin and charted a time line on each of the frontiersmen. As we recorded births, deaths, and important events, the children calculated ages, lifespans, populations, and a host of other things. History, spelling, English, social studies, art, architecture, medicine, political science, and the Bible were wrapped into this one project.

Pros

Creative: Unit studies teach in a way children are meant to learn. They stimulate their creativity and imagination and are unbeatable for the kinesthetic learner.

Time: Unit studies allow you to teach all your children at the same time and on the same subject. When it comes to written work, you simply require the older students to perform much more than the younger.

Cost: Unit studies tend to be very cost effective and work very well for large families. They allow much more flexibility than the other two approaches and employ all three learning styles to get the concepts across.

Family: The fathers can easily participate in unit studies because so many of the projects can be done in the evenings together as a family.

Cons

Time: Unit studies can require a lot of preparation time for the parents. Although the books are very cost effective, sometimes the projects suggested in them can get pricey.

Unfamiliar: They can be scary for first-time homeschoolers, and it takes years for some mothers to get over their obsession for structure. It can be difficult getting your students to complete work within a specified time frame because of the free and loose nature of the unit study.

Diploma: Unit studies are difficult to grade, so diplomas could become an issue.

Appropriate Grade Level

For some of you beginning homeschooling, you are coming into it with an older child who has already spent time in a public or private school. Before you are able to purchase the curriculum you need, you may have to determine a correct grade level for each subject. The fact that your child just came out of "third" grade means nothing when it comes to ordering material. You are going to need to get a diagnostic test to determine a correct grade level for each and every subject.

The Diagnostic Test

A diagnostic test is different from an achievement test because it is designed not only to determine the grade level of the child right down to the year and month, but it is also designed to discover any gaps in his or her education. The diagnostic may determine that your child has a reading level equal to the sixth grade but only a third grade level in spelling. The test can also determine what concepts the child has not understood and needs to go back and learn. This test is very important because public and private schools are not all teaching the same thing at the same time. It is also well known that private school and homeschooling material are much more advanced than that of the public schools.

Three companies that furnish diagnostic tests are:

Great Christian Books
P.O. Box 8000
Elkton, MD 21922-800
1-800-775-5422

Alpha Omega Publications
P.O. Box 3153
Tempe, AZ 85281
800-821-4443

ACE—Basic Education
P.O. Box 1438
Lewisville, TX 75067
800-873-3435

∞

Checklist

___ STEP ONE: I have reviewed all my options and am convicted and convinced that God would have us homeschool our children.

___ STEP TWO: I have organized and consolidated all my incoming homeschooling material into one place.

___ STEP THREE: I have purchased or put together a notebook of some kind and have transferred all my notes, addresses, etc., into it.

___ STEP FOUR: I have secured a copy of my state laws and know fully what my legal right to homeschool is.

___ STEP FIVE: I have evaluated my learning style and that of my children and have a pretty good handle on how we assimilate information.

___ STEP SIX: I have reviewed the two main approaches to education and know which direction the Lord would have my family head.

___ STEP SEVEN: I understand the three basic types of curricula available and am ready to start shopping for the one that meets the needs of my family.

Step Eight:

Purchasing Materials

The first year we began to homeschool, I had so much fun putting our school together. I bought a desk for our daughter, one for myself, a state flag, a national flag, a Christian flag, a blackboard, etc. Are you getting the picture? I tried to duplicate the only classroom I knew. Each morning my daughter and I would line up outside our schoolroom and march in together, single file (no talking in the line), address each of the flags, and say our pledges. For the most part, we played school that very first year. Since then, our schoolroom has changed dramatically.

For one thing, we no longer have just one room set aside to do school in. Although the children each have their own desks, one is in the living room with a lamp on it. One is downstairs with a computer sitting on top of it, and the other two are in my office with boards across them to make a great bookshelf. Get the picture? However, in the house we lived in prior to this one they were all put together in a neat square and definitely used for school seat work. The key is flexibility. Over the past thirteen years that we have homeschooled, we usually have ended up having school right there at our kitchen table as we are doing right now. I will use the desks or other tables in the house when the children have the giggles or can't seem to keep their eyes and hands to themselves. Having a space away, but not too far away, can particularly help the auditory learner. They seem to do better within ear reach but with space to themselves.

What Is Essential?

I am going to assume that most readers are on a budget, possibly working off of one income, and get down to what I believe are the bare essentials. I will also give you creative and inexpensive ways to secure, produce, or purchase these materials.

Furniture

A Table

The kitchen table seems to work the best in most families. Not only is it large enough to spread out on, but it is located in a place where Mom can accomplish other jobs and still maintain the school time.

Bookshelves

Someone once said at a seminar directed toward men, "If you love your wife, bring her home a bookshelf, not roses." How true. Homeschooling means books, and lots of them. We do not turn down any offers for bookcases someone wants to unload. You can make your own book-case with bricks and boards but be very careful that it is secure and little guys can't pull it down on top of them when they decide to mountain climb. You can also use stackable crates for bookshelves, giving each child his or her own cubby and color.

Cupboard

It is essential that you have one place in the house designated for school materials. Different houses will accommodate families in different ways, so try to be creative. Perhaps the following guidelines will help.

• It needs to be near the area where you will be doing your primary instruction.

• Keep the materials high enough so toddlers cannot reach them but low enough for the older children to be able to get supplies down for you.

• Hang up on the wall as much as you can to keep from using valuable drawer and shelf space. For instance, tape can use up a lot of room so I dug out an old mug rack, hung it on the wall, and now hang all my tape rolls on it. It works great for all types of tape, including masking, Scotch, electrical, and duct.

• Consider using your coat closet. Even if you put drawers or shelves on the bottom, you still have the bar to hang up short coats. If you can put the coats elsewhere, double stack a small dresser and a small set of shelves in there.

Blackboard / Whiteboard

Although we got rid of the flags from the early days, we kept the boards. The old-fashioned chalkboard works just as well as the dry-erase whiteboards. Something else to consider is using a dry-erase pen on the side of your refrigerator. It wipes right off unless what you have written remains there for an extended period of time. In that case, use a household cleaner to take off the remaining residue. I have even used a permanent marker to write things I didn't want erased and removed it later with fingernail polish remover. PLEASE NOTE: If you have an older refrigerator, doublecheck this in an inconspicuous spot before you jump right in. Some of the older appliances used paint that can absorb the marker and make it very difficult to remove.

Supplies

When I was in grade school, before the beginning of each school year, the local paper would publish what each student needed to purchase and bring to school. The following is just such a checklist for what I believe are essential supplies. You can add to it or take away from it to fit your own family's individual needs.

____ Pencils—Try buying one special pencil per child and taping his or her name on it. This is more cost-effective than buying a whole box because they will take special care of it.

____ Scissors—It is wise to have one pair per child. Again, use different colors or tape each child's name to a pair.

____ Glue—One bottle per child works well because they will tend to use it more sparingly, especially if you offer a reward at the end of the year for the child who has the most left.

____ Glue Stick—Just one should do it because this is not used as much by the children as it is by you.

____ Red Pencil or Pen—I use this daily to correct pages, make assignments, sign off on pages completed, and a host of other things. If you use just one color from the very beginning, your eyes will automatically scan for it on any page you are working with.

____ Crayons—I like to have a set of the big fat ones as well as the skinny ones. As crayons become broken, separate them out into a box to be used by the little ones that tend to break them.

____ Markers—I like to keep these in a box by themselves and bring them out only when there is adequate supervision.

____ Alphabet—I like to use a set of 8-1/2-by-11-inch letters produced by Alpha and Omega. It has a corresponding picture of an animal for each letter of the alphabet (e.g., *R* for Raccoon, *G* for Gorilla). I recommend you hang these all around the area where you do the primary teaching.

___ Box of Colored Pencils
___ Ruler
___ Yardstick
___ Reward Stickers or Stars
___ White Typing Paper
___ Colored Construction Paper
___ Scribble Pad (inexpensive newsprint paper)
___ Stapler
___ Box of Staples
___ Paper Clips
___ Map of the United States (USA students)
___ Map of the World
___ Calendar

There are many other things you could get for your work area, but I feel these items are essential. Personalize your list with what you feel your family will need.

The ages of your children will influence this list a great deal. As your children grow, the need for things such as alphabet cards will diminish.

Recommended Reading

There are some books that I strongly recommend you have as you begin your homeschooling program. Of course you are reading the first one!

1. The Bible—We have found that the Life Application Bible and the Serendipity Bible (Littleton, Colorado: Serendipity House, 1988), work the best for our family. For our daughter's last three years of school, the Serendipity was her total Bible curriculum.

2. Dictionary—The best dictionary I have had has been the *Student Handbook Including Webster's New World Dictionary, Volume I and II* (Nashville, Tennessee: The Southwestern Company, 1971). I have known of families that have homeschooled with just these two volumes and a Bible. Once you see them, you will know why.

3. Christopher J. Klicka, *The Right Choice* (Gresham, Oregon: Noble Publishing Associates, 1993). This book will give you a great deal of confidence and the ability to answer any critics concerning legal, historical, and success issues, to name a few.

4. Mary Pride, *The Big Book of Home Learning, Volumes 1-4* (Wheaton, Illinois: Crossway Books, 1990). These books are indispensable when it comes to curriculum selection.

5. *World Book Encyclopedia* early editions. You can very easily find old sets of encyclopedias at thrift shops, garage sales, and used book stores for just pennies. The older editions are the best because they are less polluted with politically correct propaganda.

There are many other books that I consider very helpful, but the above list is pretty essential. For a complete list of what I consider the cream of the crop, I refer you to "The Best of the Best" in step 18.

Checklist

___ STEP ONE: I am not only convinced to homeschool, but I am convicted by the Holy Spirit that this is God's will for my life.

___ STEP TWO: I have organized and consolidated all my incoming homeschooling material into one place.

___ STEP THREE: I have purchased or put together a notebook of some kind and have transferred all my notes, addresses, etc., into it.

___ STEP FOUR: I have secured a copy of my state laws and know fully what my legal right to homeschool is.

___ STEP FIVE: I have evaluated my learning style and that of my children and have a pretty good handle on how we assimilate information.

___ STEP SIX: I have reviewed the two main approaches to education and know which direction the Lord would have my family head.

___ STEP SEVEN: I understand the three basic types of curricula available and am ready to start shopping for the one that meets the needs of my family.

___ STEP EIGHT: I have looked over the list of supplies required for my homeschooling program and have put together or purchased what I need.

Step Nine:

Establishing Roles

Years ago, we were involved with a homeschooling curriculum that took great interest in the fathers. Dads were encouraged to take an active role in the education process. Each week we had to fill out reports on how well we did with our children, causing us to continually evaluate our parental involvement. The major problem with that program and system was that it encouraged the wife to evaluate the husband's performance weekly. A great deal of pressure was put on the husband, mine included, to use much, if not all, of his spare time to teach the children.

We had some major quarrels in those days over how much involvement my husband needed to have. Each week my expectations grew, and each week we had another fight. The quarrels would usually end up with me threatening to send our daughter to public school if my husband did not start doing more, and more and more. In looking back, I am amazed and have no idea how he did all that he did do.

The Lord began to deal with me and my attitude when one day a good friend mentioned he could never use the same program we used because he had to work for a living. What did he mean by that? Let me explain.

The Lord had blessed us with a successful business that allowed my husband to minister where needed and work inside the home. His company only needed him on a part-time basis, so he had many free hours each week, which he ended up using to teach science and math and fill out all those reports among other things. As much as my husband did, according to the program we were in and my lousy attitude, it was never enough. Terry was spending as much as thirty hours a week just doing school and school-related projects. God used our friend's statement to plant a seed in my spirit. I began to see our situation from our neighbor's eyes, and I wasn't liking what I was seeing. One day I had a long talk with my heavenly Father, asked His forgiveness, and prayed that He would cause me to rest in this particular area.

A short time later, my husband was struck with a serious heart attack, putting him in intensive care. Unknown to me at the time, Terry was having some serious discussions with the Lord on his own. Terry began to realize that although he was doing many things with his daughter, his heart wasn't in it. He was doing what was expected of him by his wife and the creators of the program, not because he desired to do so. He began to question how our daughter's life would change if he were no longer around. The answer to that made him uncomfortable. He prayed and proposed in his heart that if God allowed him to survive, he would pour his life into the children.

Terry did survive and changed in such a dramatic way. Was he taking on more responsibility with the schooling? Actually, he was doing less, but now he was doing what he felt God would have him do, and he was doing it because he wanted to, not because he had to.

About that same time, I read a great book entitled *A Survivor's Guide to Home Schooling* by Luanna Shackelford and Susan White. The Lord used this book to show me that my whole focus was wrong. I was looking at everything my husband wasn't doing rather than everything he was. He was

- providing a good income so I could homeschool.
- setting a Godly example of faithfulness and responsibility before me and the children.
- always building a shelf somewhere to keep me organized.
- supportive in every way of the decision to homeschool.

His Role

One way to understand the roles we have is to picture the father as the principal of the school and the mother as the teacher. Each has clearly defined roles.

In my opinion, let Dad do as much as he can or wants to. Do not make the same mistake I did and nag him into doing what his heart isn't into. I know of some families in which the husband delights in coming home and handling some of the subjects like math, science, history, and even art. Some men are natural teachers and use their free time in the evening to teach school, as opposed to watching TV. That kind of flexibility is the beauty of homeschooling. I guarantee those children look foreword to the time they get to spend with Dad and have a great expectation for school.

There are no set-in-stone boundaries for what Dad or Mom should be doing. Each family must address this issue on an individual basis and not be pressured to do what the "Superman Support Group Leader" does. Let the fathers work within their gifting. Terry happens to be very gifted at anything mechanical, electrical, or "woodsy"—you know, all that macho stuff. Yet, book work drives him batty. (No wonder he had so much trouble with all those reports.)

Ideas for Dad

Below are some ideas for things Dad can do to help with the homeschooling.

___ **Pray.** Depending upon his work schedule, try to pray together as husband and wife every morning and or every evening.

___ **Read.** Read to the children, preferably at night before they go to bed. Read classics like *Pilgrim's Progress* and watch the children's excitement grow each night as they anticipate what will happen next.

___ **Fix-Its.** When you have a window to fix, weather stripping to replace, or a lock to repair, plan on using it as class time with one or more of the children. Plan for it to take more time than usual so you don't get frustrated.

___ **Provide.** Be gracious when your wife tells you that she needs school material or organizational tools. Don't make her feel like she has just asked for something frivolous and unimportant. Make sure she knows it is a priority to you.

___ **Date Night.** Once a week or, at the least, every two weeks, take your wife on a date to get a progress report, allow her time to vent her frustrations, and, mostly, to reassure her that she is a priority. Some dates can be to nice restaurants; others, when the budget is tight, can be for an ice cream cone. We know one father who gets pizza for the children, gets them to bed early, and then orders out Chinese food for the two of them. They have a very relaxed date in their own living room where she is able to show him work the children have recently completed.

___ **Time Out.** Plan blocks of time, an hour here and there, when you can take the children, even the baby, on an outing to give Mom some free time.

___ **Discipline.** One father made it clear to the children that if they would not respond correctly to their mother's leadership all she had to do was call him and he would leave his job and come home that day. He says it only happens once or twice a year, but that is enough to get the message across. Dad, you need to back up the authority your wife has with the children during the day.

Her Role

In most cases, Mom is the one who does the primary teaching by virtue of the fact that she is with the children during the day. Most moms are naturals when it comes to homeschooling. I love to homeschool. I love the time I get to spend with the children. I love watching and hearing the way they think. One day, while I was working with my children, one of the boys stopped and got an unusual look on his face. I asked him what he was thinking and he replied, "I was just thinking about how much I like my bones. I like the way God put them on the inside of my skin instead of the outside because I like the way my fur feels" (he was referring to the hair on his eight-year-old arms!). He went on, "If God had put my bones on the outside I wouldn't be able to feel all this fur!" Although I am just not an emotional person by nature, I sat there and began to cry out of sheer joy and happiness at being able to get a glimpse into his blossoming brain. Moms may have the most work to do when it comes to all this homeschooling, but they certainly have the most rewards.

For most moms, their lives are so busy that the idea of taking on responsibility for the education of the children can seem overwhelming. If your glass is already full, you cannot put more into it without something spilling over. Therefore, something has to go.

A wise man once told me that "a priority is anything that will bump something else." When the phone rings during the middle of family devotions and you drop everything to get it, you have communicated to your children what your priorities are. Begin to think about what may need to be bumped in order for you to take on homeschooling.

___ **A Job.** Homeschooling usually means Mom has to give up her outside job. I have seen families who are able to have both parents work on alternating schedules, but it takes a huge commitment.

___ **Bowling League.** Bowling, softball, etc.—all those extracurricular activities need to be reevaluated.

___ **Bible Studies.** This one is tough, but some churches pull the family apart with all the individual ministries, and ladies' Bible studies can be a problem. What good would it be if you knew every missionary journey Paul took, what he had for breakfast, lunch, and dinner, and what kind of sandals he wore, but were unavailable to meet the needs of your children? Children are smart and can add up all the time we spend in church-related activities versus time we spend with them.

Remember, a priority is anything that will bump something else. The key to working out your roles is determining what your priorities are and committing to guard one another's time.

Recommended Reading

1. Luanna Shackelford and Susan White, *The Survivor's Guide to Homeschooling* (Wheaton, Illinois: Crossway Books, 1988).

2. Dr. Mary Hood, *The Relaxed Home School* (Ambleside Educational Press, 140 Bond St., Westminster, MD 21157).

Checklist

___ STEP ONE: I am not only convinced to homeschool, but I am convicted by the Holy Spirit that this is God's will for my life.

___ STEP TWO: I have organized and consolidated all my incoming homeschooling material into one place.

___ STEP THREE: I have purchased or put together a notebook of some kind and have transferred all my notes, addresses, etc., into it.

___ STEP FOUR: I have secured a copy of my state laws and know fully what my legal right to homeschool is.

___ STEP FIVE: I have evaluated my learning style and that of my children and have a pretty good handle on how we assimilate information.

___ STEP SIX: I have reviewed the two main approaches to education and know which direction the Lord would have my family head.

___ STEP SEVEN: I understand the three basic types of curricula available and am ready to start shopping for the one that meets the needs of my family.

___ STEP EIGHT: I have looked over the list of supplies required for my homeschooling program and have put together or purchased what I need.

___ STEP NINE: I have gone on a date with my husband and we have clearly defined our roles and responsibilities in our homeschool decision.

Step Ten:

Keeping a Schedule

I am one of those who loves a tight schedule. I also like puzzles, so making things fit in tiny spaces could easily become an obsession with me. Terry, on the other hand, doesn't even own a watch. Words from the wise: "Opposites attract and if both of us were the same, one of us would be unnecessary." The fact is, we must all have or keep some sort of a schedule or we would be living in chaos. How you keep your schedule will depend on what educational approach you take, as discussed in Step Six. For those wanting a fairly traditional and structured program, a detailed schedule is essential. For those taking a more relaxed approach, general guidelines will do.

Another factor affecting your schedule will be your state's homeschooling laws. Some states mandate a certain number of hours per day while others want to know how many days you educate through the year. By now you should have obtained your laws or decided to operate under a satellite school and have a basic idea of the number of days and hours you plan to homeschool.

If you haven't gotten your notebook put together yet, you could be in trouble. You are going to need that in order to put your schedule together.

Options

Weeks and Months

Decide how many official days of instruction you plan to have throughout the year. I say official because we homeschool every day in some fashion or another.

—Get a calendar that shows your whole year.

—Determine your beginning date and ending date.

—Circle or mark the days you plan to homeschool, remembering not to schedule time during holidays, special occasions, and vacation.

—Keep a running total of days per week, month, and year.

For example, if you plan to homeschool 172 days, determine when you start, which days you will take off, and when you want to finish. Remember that this is just a target plan, not something set in stone. (Be sure to use a pencil with a good eraser!) Let us look at some examples.

—Begin the day after Labor Day, homeschool for five weeks, then take one week off. Continue this pattern all year until you meet your desired finish point.

—Have year-round school having three hours of seat work a day and taking off weeks at a time for holidays.

—Educate for three months solid, then take one month off. Continue this pattern year round.

—Follow the traditional schedule by beginning around Labor Day, finishing somewhere around Memorial Day, and taking the summer off.

Days

Many states like Colorado require homeschoolers to educate 172 days a year, 4 hours per day or 20 hours per week. The key word to remember is *flexibility*. If you wanted to put in two 10-hour days, you would be operating within the law. Never forget that learning takes place every waking hour of the day. Do not limit yourself to an 8-to-3 schedule. Consider some of the following options.

—5 days a week for 4 hours each day = 20 hours

—4 days a week for 5 hours each day = 20 hours. I have used this schedule some years, leaving that fifth day for shopping and outside appointments.

—3 days a week for 6 hours each day plus one field trip for 2 hours = 20 hours.

Always remember that the state requirement tells you what the government would like to see in order to insure a proper education for your child and offers a minimum goal. Go before the Lord and ask what kind of hours and schedule He would have you set. You will discover that you will be doing a whole lot more than what the state requires, not because you need to but because you will want to.

Daily

Having a daily schedule is a must if you are all planning to survive. The children will need to have clear boundaries and direction to go by. The daily schedule must be made carefully, and all must be willing to adjust to changes as they occur. Remember, a schedule is just a guideline and can be adjusted when someone is sick, guests pop in, or for a number of other things. Let us look at a sample schedule.

6:30 to 7:00—Rise, Beds, Personal Devotions
7:00 to 8:00—Breakfast and Family Devotions
8:00 to 8:45—Bible Class
8:45 to 9:00—Penmanship
9:00 to 9:45—Math
9:45 to 10:00—Break
10:00 to 11:00—Reading
11:00 to 11:45—History
11:45 to 12:30—Lunch and Break

12:30 to 2:00—Home Skills
2:00 to 2:45—Piano Practice

You get the picture. There have been some years that we have followed a schedule like the one above, and there may come a time in the future that I will do so again. Right now, the above schedule would add more stress than we need so we are working off of something more like the following.

6:30 to 9:00—Rise, Dress, Chores, and Breakfast
9:00 to 10:00—News and current events with the "700 Club."
10:00 to 12:30—Seat Work
12:30 to 2:00—Lunch and Break
2:00 to 3:30—Additional Seat work

Whatever schedule you decide upon, be sure the children are well versed in it. You may want to assign older children to take responsibility for the younger children and make sure they get from point A to point B on time.

If you live in the city, you may consider keeping the children indoors during regular school hours. Some neighbors can get very annoyed, snoopy, and troublesome when they hear children's noises during hours they don't normally expect them. That is a sad commentary on how our society as a whole feels about children.

Recommended Reading

1. Jessica Hulcy and Carol Thaxton, *The KONOS Compass, Guidebook to the KONOS Unit Study* (Guidebook to the KONOS Unit Study, P.O. Box 1534, Richardson, Texas 75083).

2. Gayle Graham, *How to Home School* (Melrose, Florida: Common Sense Press, 1992).

Checklist

____ STEP ONE: I am not only convinced to homeschool, but I am convicted by the Holy Spirit that this is God's will for my life.

____ STEP TWO: I have organized and consolidated all my incoming homeschooling material into one place.

____ STEP THREE: I have purchased or put together a notebook of some kind and have transferred all my notes, addresses, etc., into it.

____ STEP FOUR: I have secured a copy of my state laws and know fully what my legal right to homeschool is.

____ STEP FIVE: I have evaluated my learning style and that of my children and have a pretty good handle on how we assimilate information.

____ STEP SIX: I have reviewed the two main approaches to education and know which direction the Lord would have my family head.

____ STEP SEVEN: I understand the three basic types of curricula available and am ready to start shopping for the one that meets the needs of my family.

____ STEP EIGHT: I have looked over the list of supplies required for my homeschooling program and have put together or purchased what I need.

____ STEP NINE: I have gone on a date with my husband and we have clearly defined our roles and responsibilities in our homeschool decision.

____ STEP TEN: I have sat down with my calendar and worked out a schedule for the yearly, as well as the daily, hours we want to homeschool.

Step Eleven:

Home Skills

As a little girl, I grew up in an orphanage. My role models for parenting were Catholic nuns and my "home" was a huge, four-story brick building that took up half a city block. I did not grow up learning how to do laundry or fix meals for obvious reasons. While still in grade school, I went to live with an aunt and uncle in a regular home with regular people. Since my aunt worked full-time, my sister and I learned quickly how to clean a home and do the laundry. Back then, my aunt still used the old-fashioned wringer washing machines. The clothes would wash for a time in the washer, then we would feed them through two rollers and into a tub of hot water. From there we would feed them through the wringers again into a tub of cold water. Finally we would wring them out one more time, this time into a basket that we would take outside in the summertime so we could hang them on the line. During the winter, we would use the dryer or string the clothes up all around the basement. Doing laundry was an all-day affair.

Many children grow up and get married, learning how to do these skills the hard way when they wake up one morning to discover there is nothing to wear, nothing in a can to heat up, and they can't find the ringing phone under all the debris. We do a disservice to our children when we do not train them in what I consider to be survival skills. Learning these skills are important because:

1. It prepares them to have a family of their own one day or to live alone if God so desires.

2. It teaches them how to work together with other family members for a common goal.

3. It teaches responsibility.

4. Once home skills are mastered by your children, it frees you for lesson plans and teaching.

Another valuable reason for teaching these skills to our children was revealed to me when I was pregnant with my first son. Our daughter was seven. I had five miscarriages after she was born and had been told we would never be able to have children again. The last six weeks of my pregnancy, I stayed in bed with elevated blood pressure, dependent upon caring friends and neighbors to help out with meals and housework. I stumbled upon a very important reason for teaching my children how to run a home. If for any reason Mom is out of the picture—whether she goes home to be with the Lord, has to spend time with an ailing family member, is in the hospital, or is absent for some other reason—the result would be the same. I decided then to teach what I call "survival skills" to the children so that, with or without me, the home would run smoothly.

I find, as many other parents have found, that homeschooling has actually freed up my time because of the responsibilities my children have taken on.

In our early years of homeschooling, I had only our eldest daughter to teach. When she was seven, we were expecting our second child. The thought of diapers and a busy newborn prompted me to teach Emily home skills.

I began with laundry. After a few months of learning and training in every aspect of the chore, including color separation, washing, drying, folding, and putting the clothes away, I presented her with a Certificate Of Completion for her laundry skills. I did the same thing with the dishwasher, vacuum cleaner, dusting, etc. One day a friend came to visit and watched Emily as she very carefully folded each item just taken from the dryer. Rather than praise Emily for what she had accomplished, she rebuked me for using Emily as a "slave." I was quite taken aback as she informed me that she did everything for her three children because she felt it was important that they enjoyed their childhood and that we were robbing Emily of hers. I must admit I was disturbed over her comments. After she left I relieved Emily of her job and sent her out to play. For the next few days, I took over all the chores that Emily had been given and did them myself. On the third day, Emily came to me with big tears in her eyes and said, "Mommy, why can't I do my jobs anymore? Did I do something wrong?" Ouch! It was time to rethink this one. I realized that by taking the responsibilities away from Emily, she didn't feel a part of the family anymore. She enjoyed her chores and the heaps of praise she got from me when she completed them. Not only that, she was becoming bored with all this new free time she had. I had learned a lesson. We went back to the way we believed God would have us live in our family and shrugged off the criticism. As an interesting note, that same mother came back to me about four years later and complimented me on what a responsible, hard-working girl Emily had turned out to be. She also asked my advice as to how to get her children to begin to take on some of the same responsibilities now that she was going to homeschool. I told her what I am about to tell you.

Never Do Something Your Children Can Do!

Let's Get Started

If your children have already been in a public or private school, having them home is going to be quite an adjustment. Think about all the housework you did while they were gone for six to eight hours. Now, not only are they home and expecting you to use that time to teach them, they are also making more messes that someone is going to have to clean up. For you parents, let me say that if your child does not pick up a pencil to do seat work for the first month or so, that's OK. This time should be used to readjust your whole family life and give them a crash course in home skills and organization. The following suggestions may help.

—If your children are older, have a family meeting and let them know that things are going to change. Even if your children are young, having regular family meetings to discuss and plan are great.

—Make a list of all the household responsibilities and chores.

—Label the chore for difficulty and frequency. For instance, you could set up a color or number code. A number one or a blue job could be something a child as young as two could do. A number five or a red job could be something only an older child could handle.

—Choose a skill and teach it completely to the child.

Years ago when I was a girl, I read the biography of Louisa May Alcott. She had a very creative way to teach and learn a home skill, which I decided to use someday with my children. Thanks to Louisa, this is what I did to teach Emily how to dust.

Day One. I showed her how to dust each room by giving her a dust rag and having her wipe down everything right after me. We crawled on the floor to get chair legs and stood on a stool to get picture frames.

Day Two. We went over the exact same room, only this time I let her go first and I followed her, reminding her of places she might miss.

Day Three. I counted out ten M&M's and placed them all over the room on things that needed to be dusted. I didn't tell her how many M&M's were there; it was up to her to dust and come up with the right number. If she only came back with nine, that meant she missed dusting some object. Once all the candy was found, the job was done and she ate the reward.

Day Four. Again I placed candy throughout the room and let her dust and enjoy the fruit of her labor.

Day Five. We invited company over for dinner because my house never looked so good!

The Next Week. I gave it time for some fresh dust to settle. On the first day I only put out a couple of pieces of candy. On the second day, I gave Emily her final exam by following her around and watching everything she did. For the next few weeks, dusting became her responsibility three days a week until I was sure she had mastered it.

This procedure can be used to teach any chore or home skill you have. The key is to take time to instruct thoroughly and have them repeat the skill every day until they have it down.

Once you have taught that skill, you should never have to do it again because *mastery* comes when that child is able to teach the next child that same skill.

You will be amazed to discover just how many things your little ones can do. Below are some suggestions for different age groups.

One- to Three-Year-Olds

__ Wipe down baseboards
__ Collect wastepaper baskets

__ Clear the table after a meal
__ Feed the pets
__ Dust low objects
__ Put dry bread out for birds
__ Pick up toys
__ Bring clothes to the laundry room
__ Help unload the dishwasher by handing things to an older child
__ Bring clean clothes to bedrooms
__ Fold towels
__ Set the table

Do not underestimate what these little ones can do!

Four- to Seven-Year-Olds

__ Take out the trash
__ Clean mirrors
__ Clean bathrooms
__ Dust
__ Vacuum
__ Make beds
__ Wipe down appliance fronts
__ Rinse dishes for the dishwasher
__ Load and unload the dishwasher
__ Remove cobwebs
__ Organize drawers
__ Dry dishes
__ Stack firewood
__ Wash windows
__ Hose down screens and driveways

Eight Years Old and Older

__ Help the little ones get dressed
__ Wash and dry dishes
__ Help with cooking and baking
__ Sweep and mop floors

__ Wash, dry, and hang out clothes
__ Iron
__ Mow the lawn
__ Wash the car
__ Wash down walls
__ Shovel snow

These are just a few ideas. I am sure you can add to these lists a number of things that are peculiar to your home. For instance, if you live in the country or on a farm you need to include all of those barnyard responsibilities.

Assigning the Chores

My family actually enjoys this part. Having seven children helps not only to spread the jobs out but gives the opportunity for the children to help one another get their work done so they can play together.

The Weekly Draw

We have tried many systems through the years, but I find the one that works best for me is the Weekly Draw. We have all our chores on individual cards that we place in a basket. Each child draws until they are all gone. I even let the two- and four-year-old draw their share. After the jobs are drawn, I give the children four minutes to "trade." The rules to trading are that the older children cannot take unfair advantage of the younger and that if anyone gets angry, all trading ends.

When the timer goes off, they have to bring their cards to me so I can make a list to display on the refrigerator. If at any time through the week I need someone to do a particular job, I can easily look at the list and see who drew that chore.

A method like this provides accountability because if you drew bathroom one week and didn't follow through, whoever draws it the next week is going to raise the roof.

Rotation

A rotation schedule seems to work well when you are dealing with kitchen chores. With this method, one child can tolerate loading the dishwasher one week, knowing that the next week it will be his or her turn to do the rinsing. With the rotation method, you can be sure your child is constantly getting practice at every job.

Keeping Track

Once you have taught the skills and worked out the assignment of chores to the children, you need to find a way to keep track of who has what job. It is important to be able to reward those who have done well through the week and give additional training to the ones who had a struggle. It is especially important to remember who does what so that you are not asking one of the children to do something someone else is responsible for. When this happens, you create a situation that tempts your child to talk back, complain, or throw a fit.

Chore Charts

In the back of this book, I have included a sample chore chart I drew for one of my children years ago. Chore charts are great for little ones who cannot read because you can draw a picture well enough to give them the idea of what they need to do. Each day, once they complete their chore, allow them to put a sticker or smiley face in the square. At the end of the week, you can reward them for what they have done.

Choreganizer

This system, created by Jennifer Steward, is in a class all by itself. There is nothing else like it, and I would encourage you to look into it before you try to make little cards and work out a system for yourself. She provides colorful, laminated cards with pictures of the chore on one side and a detailed list of how to do the chore on the other. She provides a way for you to display the chores and a system of rewards.

Kid's Biz

This product is a notebook/organizer for your ten-year-old or older child. It not only provides a means of recording and keeping track of assigned responsibilities, it allows your child to "contract" with you to get the work done without nagging or continual reminders.

Rewards

Positive reinforcement is so much more effective than negative consequences. Look for ways to reward the children for a job well done. Rewards down here are a continual reminder of the rewards we can look forward to in heaven. Here are some ideas.

The Hope Chests

Have the children construct three beautiful "hope chests." I recommend you make them out of pencil boxes (formally known as cigar boxes) or baskets with lids. Make these boxes as nice as you can with a design that reflects graduated importance. For instance, box number one could be pretty, box number two could be beautiful, but box number three should be exquisite. The reason is that you are going to put corresponding reward ideas in each box.

One night during family night, get ideas from the children as to the kind of rewards they would like to have. Inexpensive and pleasant rewards would be written down on pieces of paper and put into box number one. Rewards with a minimal cost and somewhat more sophistication could be placed in box number two. Box number three would be reserved for the most expensive and desirable rewards.

Here are some of the rewards our family came up with.

Hope Chest of Joy (1 to 50 points required)

___ Walk around the block on Daddy's shoulders
___ Gets to choose dessert for Sunday dinner
___ One dollar
___ Picks out video from family video library for video night
___ Wrestles with Dad
___ Bakes cookies with Mom
___ Bubble bath
___ Plays favorite game with Mom or Dad
___ One day off from a hard job
___ One extra hour on the phone through the week
___ Picks out one box of cereal at the store this week

Hope Chest of Goodness (51 to 250 points required)

___ Two dollars
___ Picks out a video from the video store to rent
___ Goes out with Mom or Dad for ice cream
___ Gets to buy one book
___ Has a friend over for the whole day
___ One day of school off
___ Chooses the menu for favorite dinner for one night
___ Picks one special treat at the grocery store (set limit)
___ One day off from all chores
___ Gets two free hours of phone time this week

Hope Chest of Love (251 points or more needed)

___ Purchases one video from the video store
___ Receives five dollars
___ Dinner out with Mom or Dad at a restaurant of your choice

__ Tickets to a sports event
__ Hair cut or styling at a salon
__ Shopping day with Mom
__ Overnight camping trip with just you and Dad
__ Night out to a movie with a friend

When you come up with the rewards you want in the box, be sure to adjust the point system accordingly. The rewards in the Chest of Love should be ones that require the child to save points each week to attain. Be careful not to make "material possessions" the most sought-after rewards.

The younger children will want to redeem their points right away. Help the older children catch a vision for working toward a desired reward. Some weeks they could spend a few of their points to draw for a simple reward but save the rest for the bigger reward.

Be careful not to set the point levels too high, which can discourage the children and cause them to lose interest. Set aside one special time each week to total points and draw for the rewards Make sure the children know you delight in dishing out the rewards as much as they enjoy receiving them.

If you use the Chore Charts, at the end of the week have the child count up each of the stickers, stars, or smiley faces, giving them practice with their math skills. Then, exchange those for an M&M, raisin, penny, or points for the hope chests.

Recommended Reading or Projects

1. Jennifer Steward's *Choreganizer* is a chore system that is carried by Great Christian Books or can be gotten through Steward Ship, 916-333-1642, P.O. Box 164, Garden Valley, California 95633.

2. Debbie Hope and Cheri Ellison's "Kid's Biz Planner" can be purchased by calling 1-800-SELF-ESTEEM or writing 24843 DelPrado Suite 491, Dana Point, California 92629.

Checklist

____ STEP ONE: I am not only convinced to homeschool, but I am convicted by the Holy Spirit that this is God's will for my life.

____ STEP TWO: I have organized and consolidated all my incoming homeschooling material into one place.

____ STEP THREE: I have purchased or put together a notebook of some kind and have transferred all my notes, addresses, etc., into it.

____ STEP FOUR: I have secured a copy of my state laws and know fully what my legal right to homeschool is.

____ STEP FIVE: I have evaluated my learning style and that of my children and have a pretty good handle on how we assimilate information.

____ STEP SIX: I have reviewed the two main approaches to education and know which direction the Lord would have my family head.

____ STEP SEVEN: I understand the three basic types of curricula available and am ready to start shopping for the one that meets the needs of my family.

____ STEP EIGHT: I have looked over the list of supplies required for my homeschooling program and have put together or purchased what I need.

____ STEP NINE: I have gone on a date with my husband and we have clearly defined our roles and responsibilities in our homeschool decision.

____ STEP TEN: I have sat down with my calendar and worked out a schedule for the yearly, as well as the daily, hours we want to homeschool.

____ STEP ELEVEN: I have made a list of all the chores and responsibilities within the home and have developed a plan to teach these skills.

Step Twelve:

Tools of the Trade

A common question homeschoolers have to deal with is how can you as a parent compete with all the advantages the public school can provide? One of the first items that comes to mind is the science lab with all its petri dishes and Bunsen burners. Good news homeschoolers; all that and more is available to you. In the early years of homeschooling a family would have been hard-pressed to come up with some of those materials, whereas now companies regularly market these items to homeschoolers. It is a matter of finding the right source.

Before we go any further, let me say that there will be trade-offs when it comes to any educational system you choose to use. You have got to weigh out what your priorities are and be willing to make sacrifices for what is most important to you. I can with great confidence claim that homeschooling is academically, socially, spiritually, and physically far superior to the public school system. In those cases where you need some specialized tutor, instrument, or piece of equipment, they can be found. You just have to know where to look.

Tutors

If you find yourself in need of specialized help in one field or another, a tutor can be just the ticket. For families that live near colleges and universities, tutors come in all sizes and talents. Some areas that you might want to find tutors for are:

- Music Lessons
- Foreign Language
- Sports
- Drama
- Journalism

For any subject that your child seems to excel in and shows a greater interest in than you feel comfortable with, find a tutor. That is what happens in the public and private schools. It is only in the early grades that one teacher can do it all. As the children get older and want to be in band, the school provides a band instructor. The same goes for the homeschooler. In those early years, parents are able to give their children a broad knowledge base, but as they grow and develop their tastes and preferences, they may need specialized help.

Many times, when looking for a tutor you need to look no further than your local support group. Remember that all those mothers and fathers were once in school and have developed talents that can be shared or traded. One computer whiz father can tutor the children of parents who are very musical, who can, in turn, tutor children in music.

Another valuable resource is the older child. The older children in the family can help give instruction to the younger ones and learn some valuable skills in the meantime. One year, my oldest daughter took on responsibility for teaching all the AWANA (Approved Workmen Are Not Ashamed) verses to her brothers. She learned how to "teach" by filling out lesson plans, working out a schedule, and juggling three age groups. I was amazed at how well she did. A family in New Zealand did just that very thing, and when the eldest daughter graduated herself, she continued working with her brothers and sisters. Now several of the neighboring farm children participate in their school, and she is the "headmistress."

Libraries

Libraries are a very important resource for you because they are economical and available. I have never met a librarian whose heart could not be turned toward my children. Librarians are there because they love books and believe in reading and learning. It is refreshing to them when eager students come in wanting to check out every book they see.

Use the library on a regular basis. I like to go on every other Friday because the library had story time then. Below are some helpful hints about library uses.

—Check out the library ahead of time because there can be unsuitable sections.

—Limit the number of books each child can take out. We have a five-book limit in our home.

—Make sure each child has the same amount before you leave. Count the books. Once I didn't count right and spent hours scouring for a book that we never had in the first place.

—Most libraries have story time on certain days.

Support Groups

Support groups can be a very beneficial network of other parents who are like-minded and sympathetic to your needs. Usually support groups meet once a month or more and provide a time when you can get with other moms and pour your heart out. Most support groups will keep you updated either by newsletters or through a mailing as to what field trips are in the works, what businesses are offering you discounts, and what curriculum fairs are in your area. A good support group will make a way for families to trade or sell unwanted or outgrown curricula.

Support groups may not be for everybody, but I would still encourage you to check one out. They usually offer enough services so that one or more will meet your needs.

Field Trips

In the orphanage I grew up in as a child, the only field trip I ever heard of was down to the clinic to get shots. Field trips were unheard of in the "olden days," whereas now they have become a regular thing. I think they are a good idea but only with some guidelines.

Years ago, I volunteered to be the field trip coordinator for our local support group. One of the first events I planned was to the Denver Museum of Natural History. The day before we were scheduled to go, a mom gave me a call and said something had come up and she would not be able to come after all, but that her son was so looking forward to it. Was there any way he could tag along with me? Well, sure. Why not? Not long after that call, another mom called with a very similar story and request. Too make a long story short, the next day I went on a field trip with a total of four moms and thirty-four children. What a disaster! To begin with, two of the moms were starved for fellowship and spent the entire five hours and forty-two minutes talking to each other about everything from getting gum out of the carpet to a thousand and one things to do with ground beef. The other mom and I chased thirty-four children through that entire museum, praying all the while that they would not break something over one thousand years old. The only thing the children got out of it was a lot of exercise and a sack lunch in the park. That experience convinced us that the only field trips we would take in the future would be with our own family, alone! There have been a few times that we went with one other family, but it was always with a family who was like-minded with us.

The purpose of a field trip is to learn and experience something new, together as a family. Some can do that with a dozen other moms and three dozen other children, but I cannot.

While in New Zealand, we were told about an ice cream factory that gave excellent tours. As a school project, Emily designed the Field Trip Record you will find at the back of the book. After designing the sheet, she called the Tip Top Ice Cream Factory and made all the arrangements for a tour. She kept the sheet with her and filled it out while we experienced the trip. Since then, we have used those Field Trip Records for other field trips and kept a file of them for when people call and ask what we thought of such and such. I recommend that you let your children do the same, either using our sheet or designing their own.

Sports Clubs

An often expressed concern is over what homeschooled children can do in the team sports department. Thirteen years ago when we first began to homeschool, you could count on one hand the number of support groups there were in an entire state. Now you have more than that just in the suburbs of Denver. The homeschooling community has exploded, and with that have come many children. So many, in fact, that homeschool support groups have begun to form their own sports leagues that play real games with real competition. This movement has grown to the point that National Playoffs are held in Estes Park, Colorado, every year.

In some communities, the private schools will even compete with the homeschooling sports teams. Every year the homeschoolers make more and more inroads, paving the way for the next generation.

Let me caution you about placing too much importance on the competitive sports concept. As a homeschooler, you are open to a variety of options.

—Archery
—Fencing
—Golf
—Shooting
—Tennis

Consider introducing your children to sports which allow them to compete with themselves, each week improving upon last week's record.

Another caution I would offer is to examine the time factor when getting involved in competitive sports. Years ago, good friends of ours, a family with ten children, got involved in a homeschooling sports group. Their children were very gifted athletically and enjoyed all the sports offered. The time commitment for them was staggering. Because of the age differences, the children were in two different leagues, one having practices on Tuesday, the other on Wednesday. Not only were there group practices, there were also private lessons and then the actual games. On Tuesday, Thursday, and Friday they would all get into the car at 10:00 in the morning with their school work and be gone until 6:00 in the evening. During that time, they were driving sometimes as much as one hour one way to get to one field to drop off some children, then to another across town, back again for lessons, to the park for lunch, then a game. This went on for three years before Mom and Dad said "Enough." They have been able to creatively find alternatives, which included having some children play with a public school team in their area.

The courts have ruled that public schools must allow homeschool students to enroll in and participate in sports and music classes along with any other class they wish. Again, consider carefully the trade-off. Will your child benefit from the activities more than they will be harmed?

Games

Another overlooked tool in your home is that whole closet of games. Games are a wonderful way to communicate with your child. Why can't our children learn and have fun doing so in the process? Try planning on incorporating one game a week into your school schedule. It gives your children something to look forward to. Just about any good game can be used as a teaching tool and some of my favorites are the following:

—Pilgrim's Progress
—Bible Bingo
—Pictionary
—Yahtzee (great way to reinforce times tables)
—Life
—Chess
—Memory
—Parcheesi
—Trivial Pursuit
—Outburst
—The Ungame
—Triaminoes
—Boggle
—Monopoly

Probably the best loved "game" in our home is Store. On store days we do not plan any other seat work for the children. The concept is simple. The children designate one place, usually one of their rooms to be the store. They select items of all kinds and set them up in their room. They establish prices for each item, then they are open for business. Mom and Dad come in with play money and purchase what we want. Such a simple little project reaps bountiful rewards and object lessons.

The children learn:

—How to display items in their best possible light
—Toys that are broken or missing pieces are of less value
—God has abundantly blessed them with things
—How to count back change
—How to spell correctly on the price tags
—How to be courteous to customers
—To treat others fairly and with respect

There are so many other lessons to be learned. Once the store is closed, the children have an opportunity to deep clean and reorganize their room. They can also take this time to sort through and discard broken items.

Apprenticeship Opportunities

Homeschoolers are not bound by traditional school hours, which makes apprenticeship an attractive option. Look for businesses within your community that would be willing to train your older child in a given profession. Even if the child has no intention of pursuing that field for the rest of his or her life, they can greatly benefit from the experience.

Inge Cannon, a well-known figure among home-schoolers, has developed a ministry in this field. Inge sells tapes that address the subject of apprenticeships in great detail and would be worth checking into.

Recommended Reading and Programs

1. Inge Cannon, "Education Plus" (tapes), P.O. Box 1029, Mauldin, South Carolina 29662, 803-281-9316.

Checklist

____ STEP ONE: I am not only convinced to homeschool, but I am convicted by the Holy Spirit that this is God's will for my life.

____ STEP TWO: I have organized and consolidated all my incoming homeschooling material into one place.

____ STEP THREE: I have purchased or put together a notebook of some kind and have transferred all my notes, addresses, etc., into it.

____ STEP FOUR: I have secured a copy of my state laws and know fully what my legal right to homeschool is.

____ STEP FIVE: I have evaluated my learning style and that of my children and have a pretty good handle on how we assimilate information.

____ STEP SIX: I have reviewed the two main approaches to education and know which direction the Lord would have my family head.

____ STEP SEVEN: I understand the three basic types of curricula available and am ready to start shopping for the one that meets the needs of my family.

____ STEP EIGHT: I have looked over the list of supplies required for my homeschooling program and have put together or purchased what I need.

____ STEP NINE: I have gone on a date with my husband and we have clearly defined our roles and responsibilities in our homeschool decision.

____ STEP TEN: I have sat down with my calendar and worked out a schedule for the yearly, as well as the daily, hours we want to homeschool.

____ STEP ELEVEN: I have made a list of all the chores and responsibilities within the home and have developed a plan to teach these skills.

____ STEP TWELVE: I have looked over the list of tools available to me within my area and plan to schedule them in or utilize them in my program.

Step
Thirteen:

The Fast Track

Every week after one of our radio broadcasts, I get an average of four to six calls a day from parents wanting to know how to get started in homeschooling. That is a big reason why this book has been written. Many parents are ready for this option but have no clue as to how to begin.

Frequently, the calls are coming from families who have already been in the private or public school system and are ready to pull their children out *now*. They haven't got time to do all the investigating that other parents would have. If this describes you, then you need to understand how to get onto the fast track. Take the following steps, bypassing some of the other chapters in this book. Once you have successfully gotten your children out of the school and into your home, you can get back to the rest of the book.

Do Not Panic!

If you are one of those parents removing your child because of a crisis situation, stay calm. Take methodical, rational steps and everything will be fine. Some issues must be addressed *before* you make your move to prevent devastating consequences.

Begin right now to gather the prayer support you will need to proceed. I love it when I hear of a family of faith acting on the leading of the Holy Spirit to do something different with their children. It takes great courage and strength of your convictions.

1. The very first thing to do before you contact any school official is to secure a copy of your state's homeschooling laws and requirements as I discussed in Step Four. Once you know what your state requires, you can proceed. This information can probably be obtained through your state homeschooling organization listed in Step Four. Call them and they will put you in touch with homeschoolers in your area to give you further assistance.

2. Consider applying to be a member of the Home School Legal Defense Association (HSLDA) right away. Because your children are already in the public school system, some uninformed school official may try to keep you in the system by fear and intimidation.

3. Investigate your state laws to see if there is a provision for a "satellite" school. In some states, you can enroll in a private school that operates as a satellite school for homeschoolers. These private schools are not usually regulated by state laws and allow for all the teaching to take place in the home. If this option is available to you, you can go to your school administrator and tell them your child will be enrolled in a private school and have the school transfer the child's records. This option is particularly attractive to parents with children who have been diagnosed with some sort of learning disability. Schools receive extra funding for these students, so they can be reluctant to give them up.

4. Once the children have been taken out of school, have them tested with a diagnostic test. A diagnostic test will tell you exactly where the child is in every subject area. These tests are available through different curriculum providers and satellite schools and are absolutely

necessary for you to have. You cannot assume that just because your child sat in a classroom that had "4th Grade" written over the door jamb that he or she can do fourth grade level work. A diagnostic test may show that he is at 4. 2 (fourth year, second month) in math, 3.5 in reading, and 5.1 in language. Once you know where your children are, you can begin to order curricula.

5. Once you have taken the above steps, you can begin to go through this book from the beginning.

Recommended Helps and Reading

1. Diagnostic Test from Great Christian Books: 1-800-775-5422.

2. Diagnostic Testing through Christian Cottage Schools: 1-303-688-6626.

3. Home School Legal Defense Association: 1-703-338-2733.

Step Fourteen:

Streamline Schooling on a Budget

For many families, that second income has been sacrificed in order for Mom or, in some cases, Dad to be able to stay home and educate the children. This is more than a whim or a fad. When a decision you make directly hits you in the pocketbook, you become a testimony to others about what you value. It also sends a resounding message to your children about what a priority they are. You would be hard-pressed to find a child who would prefer a Nintendo to Mom being home with him. In this day and age, our children have been told in every way possible that they are of very little value. Homeschooling your child at great sacrifice financially speaks volumes to him.

There is a misconception about how expensive homeschooling can be compared to the "free" public school. Let's explore that myth.

A friend of mine who had homeschooled her children for years decided to let her junior-high age son attend the public school after he begged for months to be on their sports team. They lived in a small farming community where everyone knew each other, so she began to think it would be fairly safe. She was convinced to let him try it for one year when some unexpected bills arrived about the same time she needed to order next year's homeschooling material.

About four months later, she confided in me that it was one of the costliest decisions she had ever made. The biggest expense was the new wardrobe her son now had to have. His old clothes were not "cool" enough for school, nor were there enough of them because these days kids know if you have worn the same outfit twice in a two-week period. Sack lunches were out and fast food was in so her son needed lunch money each day. The physical education department required money for all the gym and track suits, not to mention the fact that kids in P.E. these days don't just do exercises. They now ski, scuba dive, bowl, play golf, and other outlandish things that the parents have to pick up the tab for. Add in book fees, lab fees, art fees, music fees, medical physicals for sports, class rings, yearbooks, and school pictures, and this "free" public education will break you. After adding up all the hidden costs, she figured it cost her five times what it would have cost her to homeschool. If that were not bad enough, he began to come home with attitudes and ideas each week that took hours for the family to work through.

Yes, there are costs associated with homeschooling, and parents need to be prepared to sacrifice for those things. Ask God to show you what you have available to invest into your children's homeschooling and begin there. I have seen parents that have no problem ordering out pizza a couple of times a month yet can never seem to come up with enough for a history book.

Does being on a budget mean your child has to suffer academically? Absolutely not! With relatively few resources, you can give your child an education that will gain him entrance into the most prestigious schools in the country. Here are some suggestions you might find helpful or that may stimulate your creative juices and cause you to come up with something even better.

Course Ideas

Bible

The curriculum producers have done an excellent job in coming up with some pretty elaborate Bible courses. If you want to purchase these, I remind you again to check out the doctrine and use the Curriculum Evaluation Sheet provided for you at the back of this book. This is one area in which you can save money and get a tailor-made program to boot.

I would venture to say there isn't a Bible course made that you agree 100 percent with, so this is your opportunity to make your own.

—Pray and ask God to give you a passage of Scripture to study
—Pick up a Scribble Pad (inexpensive newsprint)
—Tear off three sheets and fold in half
—Staple in the middle to form a book with six sheets of paper

You now have the book you need to study, memorize, illustrate, and write out Scripture.

Years ago, the Lord asked us to memorize Proverbs, chapter 15 as a family. We divided the chapter by five verses and began the book. We chose the title "Kindness Spoken Here" for the first five verses and went to work.

The children illustrated the cover and on the inside of the front cover they wrote out verse one. Use your judgment, but for the youngest ones I wrote the verse; the next age up copied the verse onto his page; and the oldest children wrote the verse from dictation. While they were writing the verse, I carefully explained each and every word of "A soft answer turns away wrath but a harsh word stirs up anger." We had a great discussion while they wrote out the verse, and when they were done they were told to illustrate what they had just written. You will simply be amazed at how well your children can understand and grasp the verse when given the opportunity to draw the meaning or concept.

While they are illustrating the verse, I like to create a tune to go with the verse to make it easier to memorize. In the background I sing it over and over while watching them draw, and soon they are singing it with me. I will sing it with the children three times throughout the day, and they will have it memorized by the time their heads hit the pillow. The next morning we review that verse, repeat the procedure, and do the same thing for verse two. I find that the children can easily memorize one verse a day, but after the second week, we need to have a review session. On the third week, we do not memorize new verses. Instead, we reinforce the old ones.

The benefits to doing this are (1) you control the doctrine they are learning, (2) it is less costly, (3) the children have a treasure to look back on, and (4) many verses can be memorized through the year.

When we illustrate the verses I like to give them a variety of ways to accomplish that, so each day we use a different method. I may use . . .

___ Pictures cut out from old magazines
___ Colored pencils
___ Markers
___ Crayons
___ Rubber stamps
___ Paint
___ Stencils

Not only are you teaching the Bible, but you are giving them art, spelling, and penmanship at the same time.

Serendipity

Another excellent tool for teaching the Bible is the Serendipity Bible that I wrote about in an earlier chapter. This Bible can be used as your entire Bible curriculum every year because of its format. It has actual studies created throughout that are unique in that they have many questions with no answers. This Bible stimulates your critical thinking skills masterfully without pressing you in a particular direction doctrinally. It also provides practical application to your personal life through every passage.

You can use the ready-made studies or simply assign a book, such as the Book of John. The Bible has Open, Dig, and Reflect questions that your child can answer in a separate notebook.

Open

The Open questions will ask you questions related to life. For example, in the story of the feeding of the five thousand, the question is asked, "Do you prefer to socialize at large parties, dinner for four, or a quiet evening to yourself?"

Dig

After you read the passage of Scripture that tells how the five thousand were fed, the Dig questions have you answer questions about the verses themselves, such as "Why did the crowd follow Jesus? What did they think of Him?"

Reflect

The Reflect questions bring practical application of the Scriptures to your life with questions such as "When have you seen God stretch your limited resources far beyond what you could have imagined?"

Although some of the questions may be advanced for first through third graders to work out on their own, they can easily be brought up and discussed during family devotion time.

General Knowledge

I can usually find an old set of encyclopedias on a garage sale shopping spree for literally pennies. Over the years I have acquired over ten sets that I have never had trouble finding homes for. I like using the older volumes because in many ways they are still wholesome. We will select a letter and begin at the beginning by all laying down and looking at the picture. I will take the first entry and give a synopsis. If the person or subject is particularly interesting, we will spend more time on it and even look up related stories. For instance, in one volume we came to "minerals," with a page or two of beautifully pictured rocks. Although the rock with gold in it wasn't the prettiest, it captured their attention, so we began to look in related volumes and learned all about mining, gold processing, and gold in other countries.

Later, they were allowed to write a story about gold. For this, I purchased spiral notebooks at the beginning of the year, buying a different color for each child. In this notebook the youngest ones, even the one- and two-year-olds, are allowed to draw and color to their heart's content. The older ones use this to write essays and stories. They will write the story on one side of the page and again illustrate it on the other. The words are written double-spaced so I can get in there when they are done and underline misspelled words and make grammar corrections. The children then take these books and make all the corrections, transferring the final draft to another spiral notebook, without drawings.

Take the misspelled words and use them as their spelling words for a week. Let them say them orally, write them on the board, or type them on the computer. Let them do whatever they like, because it will help them imprint those words in their memory banks.

Do not be afraid that by doing something like this they are going to miss learning about a subject at the right time. Even the professional educators cannot always agree on what needs to be taught when, so do not worry. Teach to their interests. The most important thing about it is that you are right there with them, ooing and aahing over the things you are all discovering—or in your case, rediscovering—together.

Dictionaries

Dictionaries are perhaps one of the most unused or misused resources around. We see them as things to use just to look up misspelled words, when in truth most dictionaries can be a curriculum in themselves. One dictionary in particular is *The Student Handbook* published by the Southwestern Company. It has two volumes, the first one being for the younger students and the second being for high school and college.

One-third of this dictionary is filled with information that you could teach from for many years. Science, history, geography, and every other discipline is taught in this book. The key is knowing how to teach from it. This is where prayer and creativity on your part can bring forth some of the best curricula money could buy.

Here is an example of an inexpensive geography curriculum.

—Buy an inexpensive spiral notebook, one for each continent.
—Choose one continent to begin with.
—Using one page per country, draw to scale.
—Work out a key (symbols to represent mountains, trees, etc.).
—Have your child put the symbols on the map using color.

—Include information on population, capitals and major cities, landscape, principal language and religion in regions, and chief economic production.
—Working through one continent a year is realistic.
—Let each child work at his or her own pace, encouraging them to pay close attention to detail.

All the information you need is in *The Student Handbook* dictionary but encourage the children to use an encyclopedia to gather additional facts.

Above all, do not be afraid to experiment and be creative. The first step is to pray about the educational needs of your children and ask the Lord to give you the ideas. Almost all the ideas I have come up with have come that way; only a few were things I saw other families doing. That is certainly not to my credit but to the Lord and His Spirit, who will give you the wisdom you need when you need it. Just ask Him!

Recommended Reading

1. Valarie Bendt, *How to Create Your Own Unit Study* (Tampa, Florida: Common Sense Press, 1990).

2. Jessica Hulcey and Carol Thaxton, *KONOS Compass and Curriculum* (Richardson, Texas: n.p., n.d.).

Checklist

___ STEP ONE: I am not only convinced to homeschool, but I am convicted by the Holy Spirit that this is God's will for my life.

___ STEP TWO: I have organized and consolidated all my incoming homeschooling material into one place.

___ STEP THREE: I have purchased or put together a notebook of some kind and have transferred all my notes, addresses etc., into it.

___ STEP FOUR: I have secured a copy of my state laws and know fully what my legal right to homeschool is.

___ STEP FIVE: I have evaluated my learning style and that of my children and have a pretty good handle on how we assimilate information.

___ STEP SIX: I have reviewed the two main approaches to education and know which direction the Lord would have my family head.

___ STEP SEVEN: I understand the three basic types of curricula available and am ready to start shopping for the one that meets the needs of my family.

___ STEP EIGHT: I have looked over the list of supplies required for my homeschooling program and have put together or purchased what I need.

___ STEP NINE: I have gone on a date with my husband and we have clearly defined our roles and responsibilities in our homeschool decision.

___ STEP TEN: I have sat down with my calendar and worked out a schedule for the yearly, as well as the daily, hours we want to homeschool.

___ STEP ELEVEN: I have made a list of all the chores and responsibilities within the home and have developed a plan to teach these skills.

___ STEP TWELVE: I have looked over the list of tools available to me within my area and plan to schedule them in or utilize them in my program.

___ STEP THIRTEEN: I have looked over the fast track section and have taken appropriate steps for my child (where appropriate).

___ STEP FOURTEEN: I have worked out a budget and feel I can create the things that I cannot purchase at this time.

Step Fifteen:

Home Industries

The previous chapter dealt with homeschooling on a budget. Now let us look at ways we can increase that budget. Home industries are not only common among homeschooling families, they are very successful. Our radio program was begun as a ministry but has now become a home industry. Even the book you are reading has sprung up from the same concept.

In 1984 while still in Bible college, my husband began a mobile emissions company in the Denver area. His reasons for starting it were very biblical. His number one goal was to provide an income base for ministry and missions. Our philosophy: Don't ask others to do for you, what you can do for yourself. Sensing that someday we would be serving the Lord as missionaries, we wanted to have a "tent-making" ministry whereby we were able to work and minister at the same time. Another reason for beginning the business was to test the biblical principles of finance that we were seeing in God's Word. Previously, we had owned successful businesses in Arizona. I say successful, but only by the world's standards. They made a great deal of money, but they nearly cost us our marriage and walk with the Lord. They were established with worldly ideas, concepts, and goals. Now we had an opportunity to try something God's way. One final reason for beginning the business was to provide a means of employment and training for the young people in our church.

God richly blessed our business, and in a couple of short years it grew to be the largest mobile emissions company in the state. We had learned a great deal from that business, were allowed ministry opportunities, and were able to begin other home industries as a result. The first home industry to develop actually began as a school project for my daughter.

The Chicken or the Egg?

After moving onto a hobby farm on the outer edge of Denver, we bought twenty-four laying hens as a school project for my then ten-year-old daughter. We were trying to teach her some simple math and accounting principles, so we told her that she could have all the proceeds from the sale of the eggs if she were to take on the total care and responsibility of the chickens. We helped her build a hen house and nesting and food boxes. After the hens adjusted and she had eggs to sell, we showed her how to do some simple accounting. She learned to figure out percentages as she put money aside for savings and tithing, and we taught her how to buy the grain and supplies she needed.

So many wonderful benefits came from this simple math project. It grew to be one of the largest free-range chicken businesses in the Denver area, and when we left Colorado in 1990 for New Zealand, she had over three hundred layers. She had more customers than she had eggs and financially she benefited greatly. All that from a simple math project.

During that period of time we actually had sixteen home industries that we operated as a ministry. Our emissions business provided well for our income, so we were able to use these other home industries to minister to other people.

If you are thinking about beginning a home industry, I recommend you consider some simple guidelines.

1. Ask God. This may sound religious to you, but nevertheless it really is something you should think about. Too often we jump right into something because we have seen it work for someone else. We have got to always consider God's will and know for sure that He wants this for us.

2. Determine your purpose and goal. Why do you want a home business?

— Extra money
— Fame
— Ministry
— Character builder
— Time filler
— Economical gifts

There is nothing wrong with wanting extra money as long as you have godly reasons and purposes for those finances. Some families take all the income from their home businesses and give it to ministries or missionaries. Others have used that income to bring Dad home and allow them to work together as a family.

3. Research your home business as a part of school. Some home industries require permits, home inspections, licenses, or approval from city hall. If you have gone before the Lord and feel He wants you to consider a particular business as a home industry, find out everything you can about it and develop your children's research skills in the process. Be sure to check out your loan at the bank if you are purchasing your home. Some lending institutions prohibit you from operating a business from your home under penalty of law. I know of one family who inadvertently found out that a home business would violate the terms of their loan, so they refinanced the house and secured a new loan with a new lender.

Some home businesses that involve other people's children may require you to have your home inspected by city, county, state, or federal employees. When you begin to find out about all the hoops you need to jump through for one particular business, you may change your mind. Do the research before you invest your resources into the project.

4. Try to find a home business that is essential. By that, I mean something that would still be needed if there were a national financial crunch. When times get tough, people are less likely to visit tanning salons, so find a business that would be needed should there be a recession.

Let's review some options:

—**Animal Boarding:** If you have some extra acreage, consider building dog runs or horse stalls and begin to board animals. People going on vacation are always looking for a reliable, responsible person to care for their pets.

—**Animal Breeding:** If you are going to have a dog, get one that could possibly bring in some money upon the sale of her pups.

—**Animal Grooming:** The children could learn a great deal about animals when involved in this business.

—**Auto Mechanics:** When times get tough financially, people fix their old car instead of buying a new one.

—**Calligraphy:** Look at how many handwritten signs there are in every store. A quarter a word adds up in a big hurry.

—**Catering:** Years ago a friend of mine was asked to cater a rehearsal dinner for a wedding. She did a terrific job, had fun, and made money to boot!

—**Ceramics:** I know of one woman who makes pots all day long. She sells her completed work to large department stores and makes a good living.

—**Chair Caning:** I know of another woman who had a great set of caned chairs. When one broke, she sat down and worked with the chair until she figured it out. Now she fixes chairs from all over the country.

—**Child Care:** This is so needed, very dangerous and could put your children at risk. However, children need us, and if God says do it, just do it.

—**Computer Programming:** This became one of our home industries after we computerized our emissions business. My husband discovered he had a knack for it, so other businesses hired him to help them with theirs.

—**Cooking:** This is one business that may require you to have your kitchen inspected. We began to bake freshly ground whole wheat bread that people were willing to pay $3.50 a loaf for.

—**Crafts:** This is not always a big money maker but it will bring your family closer together and save you money when it comes to holiday gift giving.

—**Furniture Refinishing:** You can very easily contract out to antique stores or used furniture shops.

—**Garden:** I know of some families that had more garden space than they needed, so they rented garden space to friends and neighbors. Their children were then paid to weed and water.

—**House Cleaning:** This home industry actually moves out of your home but can be a very profitable business.

—**Ironing:** My daughter enjoyed ironing and earned one dollar a shirt five years ago. I imagine that rate has gone up some since then.

—**Jewelry Making:** This was a hobby for a relative of mine until it began to pay more than he received as a teacher at a junior college.

—**Home Sales Parties:** Cosmetics, toys, wicker, food storage units, vitamins, and many other products are being sold through home parties.

—**Photography:** A friend of ours in New Zealand did photography as a hobby and was able to sell photos to calendar and puzzle companies. One of her photographs was on the official Red Cross Donor Card for all of New Zealand.

—**Picture Framing:** This has become more and more popular over the years and can be done with very little investment.

—**Recycling Shop:** Used clothing, books, and furniture can all be converted to cash if you know what you are doing.

—**Sell an Idea:** My husband read about a man who had an idea for a gadget that, when installed in your engine, would give your car great performance and gas mileage. All he did was offer to sell the idea in magazines around the country and ended up with over $250,000 after expenses. When customers sent him $19.95, he sent them the "idea" on a piece of paper.

—**Sewing:** Sewing has become very popular as a hobby, but some of the great mending and repair skills are disappearing. As long as we rip clothing, there will be a need for a seamstress.

—**Toy Making:** Grandpas do it as a hobby for fun and are discovering that there is quite a market for wooden, solidly built toys.

—**Tutoring:** This job is earning homeschoolers a great deal of money all over the country.

—**Typing:** If you live around a college or university, this could be a great source of income. The students arrive every year with more money than they have skills. You can capitalize on that!

—**Window Washing:** Of all the jobs listed, this one will give you the best return on your financial and time investment.

—**Writing:** We will personally see how financially viable this home industry could be in a few months from now.

These are just a few ideas to stimulate your own creative juices. God bless as you consider the right home industry for you.

Recommended Reading

1. *The Busy Woman's Daily Planner* by Heritage House and Dinah Monohan.

2. Donna Partow, *Homemade Business—A Woman's Step-By-Step Guide to Earning Money At Home* (Colorado Springs, Colorado: Focus on the Family Publishing, 1992).

3. Joanne Cleaver, *Work at Home Options* (Elgin, Illinois: David C. Cook Publishing Co., 1994).

Checklist

___ STEP ONE: I am not only convinced to homeschool, but I am convicted by the Holy Spirit that this is God's will for my life.

___ STEP TWO: I have organized and consolidated all my incoming homeschooling material into one place.

___ STEP THREE: I have purchased or put together a notebook of some kind and have transferred all my notes, addresses, etc., into it.

___ STEP FOUR: I have secured a copy of my state laws and know fully what my legal right to homeschool is.

___ STEP FIVE: I have evaluated my learning style and that of my children and have a pretty good handle on how we assimilate information.

___ STEP SIX: I have reviewed the two main approaches to education and know which direction the Lord would have my family head.

___ STEP SEVEN: I understand the three basic types of curricula available and am ready to start shopping for the one that meets the needs of my family.

___ STEP EIGHT: I have looked over the list of supplies required for my homeschooling program and have put together or purchased what I need.

___ STEP NINE: I have gone on a date with my husband and we have clearly defined our roles and responsibilities in our homeschool decision.

___ STEP TEN: I have sat down with my calendar and worked out a schedule for the yearly, as well as the daily, hours we want to homeschool.

___ STEP ELEVEN: I have made a list of all the chores and responsibilities within the home and have developed a plan to teach these skills.

___ STEP TWELVE: I have looked over the list of tools available to me within my area and plan to schedule them in or utilize them in my program.

___ STEP THIRTEEN: I have looked over the fast track section and have taken appropriate steps for my child (where appropriate).

___ STEP FOURTEEN: I have worked out a budget and feel I can create the things that I cannot purchase at this time.

___ STEP FIFTEEN: I have read the section on home industries and have some ideas about a future home industry for my family.

Step
Sixteen:

Branching Out

You are coming down the home stretch now and should be feeling pretty comfortable with what you are doing or about to do with your homeschooling program. Once you get into the swing of things, this chapter will make more sense to you and have greater appeal.

I have always enjoyed watching figure skaters perform. They have such grace and daring at the same time. The first time I got on a pair of skates, I tried to imitate the skaters I had seen on the television and ended up on the ice in a very unladylike pose. The first step to ice skating is putting on the skates, and doing a triple axle is perhaps the final step, but there are a whole lot of steps in-between. When we try to skip over all those important steps, such as learning how to stand, stop, and skate backwards, we end up in an embarrassing heap, flat on our faces.

The same thing applies to homeschooling, and that is why I arranged these chapters in graduated steps. Some of the steps can be switched around without bringing confusion; however, be careful to do the essentials before taking on anything extra.

As you feel comfortable with your homeschooling program, begin to branch out in some of the following areas.

Computers

Contrary to what some people believe, it is not necessary for you to have a computer to home educate. As nice as they are, they are still optional. When you begin to look around for a computer, do not be afraid to get an older model if you can get a great deal.

Many computer companies are taking traded-in computers and hauling them off to the dump because they have no real resale value. If you cannot afford a new computer, find one you and the children can cut your teeth on. Then begin to save for something better in the future.

Our first computer was an Adam. If you have never heard of Adams, don't feel too bad. They stopped producing the Adams in the eighties, which may explain why we purchased our first computer for $199.00 instead of $699.00. This obsolete computer turned out to be the best investment we ever made. My husband used it to finish all the college papers that eventually earned him his B.A.

Of course, if you can afford a new computer look for something with CD ROM capability. The software for these things are incredible and wonderful educational tools.

Ministry

Homeschooling is a means to an end, not an end in itself. Use your homeschooling to find the ministry God wants you to have. When you begin homeschooling, you will eventually have time to spare and use to minister to others. Ministry opportunities should be included in your lesson planning because they are a vital part of your program.

Each year we had our oldest daughter pick an area of service or ministry to work on. For several years she was a junior staff aid with the American Red Cross. Although she was there to serve and help, she learned valuable office skills at the same time. Another year she worked as a volunteer at a nursing home, giving one-on-one attention to a lady with no family.

A very special ministry opportunity came to us in an unusual way. A woman in our church had just had her third child; all of her children were under four years of age. She was overwhelmed and discouraged. She was a very good mother whose time seemed to be consumed with these little guys, partly because her husband had just begun his own business, requiring him to be out of the home for long hours. At the same time, Emily was wanting to do some outside baby-sitting, not just baby-sitting for her brothers. God gave us an idea that we presented to the new mother. We explained that Emily wanted to learn baby-sitting skills outside the home, and all we needed was a mom willing to leave her house for four hours one morning a week to let her learn. We would be available, of course, and this would be a school project, so there would be no charge for the baby-sitting services. This mother graciously agreed and Emily began her new course, Baby-sitting 101.

Here was an opportunity to combine ministry with a great educational experience. Each week Emily prepared a snack for the children, earning home skill credits, and prepared a Bible verse and story. On Thursday mornings I would drive her to the family's home and drop her off, picking her up three hours later. At that time we would go out for an ice cream cone and discuss all that she did and any problems she had. Then we would make plans for the next week. Later that year, when we felt God saying it was finally time to go to New Zealand, the one and only concern Emily had about leaving was who would take care of her "family." As it turned out, another homeschooling family in the church decided to continue the baby-sitting ministry that Emily had begun.

Ministry opportunities are everywhere if you just open your spiritual eyes to them. Consider some of the following:

—Minister to an elderly person in your neighborhood
—Junior staff aid for the Red Cross
—Baby-sitting for a single parent
—Tutoring a younger child
—Doing yard work for an elderly couple
—Visits to a nursing home

Learning Disabilities

Can you tell me what a learning disability is? Everywhere I go, just about every other call I get is from someone whose child has been diagnosed as learning disabled (LD). The parents are held hostage by the professionals who have convinced them that only the schools are equipped to teach these children. If that is true, how do you explain the fact that my daughter can read, write, operate a computer, and run my home better than I can without the benefit of ever having been in public school?

I submit to you that in the truest sense of the word, we are all learning disabled. We all have abilities to learn quickly in some areas and slowly in others. What about . . .

• the accountant who cannot locate the dip stick in order to check the oil?
• the valedictorian who cannot work the register at Wal-Mart?
• the football player unable to figure his taxes?

As we discovered with our daughter, she could learn once we found the right message center to go through. I remember spending hours and hours with her trying to help her learn her colors only to have her forget them by the next morning. One day her speech therapist suggested that on the long drive down to her office we should point out the color of each stop light we passed. Was it green, red, or yellow? It took weeks, but she did learn those three colors that way. As for the other colors, the Lord gave us an idea. One morning we woke her up and told her it was a pink day. We dressed her in pink, put pink ties in her hair, put pink dye in the pancake batter, used a pink crayon to color with all day, and made pink play dough. All day long it was pink day, and we looked for ways to remind her of that. We would have one color day a week, and it didn't take long for her to finally catch on. We found the key was in knowing our daughter and understanding what she could and couldn't do, what she liked and didn't like, and trying to make learning as much fun as possible.

The idea we had for a "color" day came from the Lord and our understanding of our daughter and out of a need she had to learn colors. It did not come from a book. Even the experts in the special education field will tell you they do much of their teaching by trial and error. They find that one thing works well for one student while something else works better for another.

It is my personal belief that many of the children labeled as LD have come down with a bad case of a teacher with a teaching disability. Teachers are coming out of college not being taught how to teach. They may try one approach on thirty children that gets through to maybe half. Does that mean that the other half are learning disabled? Could the fact that the school districts get an increase in funding for any student so labeled, have anything to do with the dramatic rise in numbers?

I am just a mom, so who am I to think that a child who can sit for three hours in front of a television, video or arcade game with no problems, yet in school is labeled as having attention deficit disorder, may be misdiagnosed?

Because of our workshop and radio ministry, we get many visits from parents seeking help and advice. While in New Zealand I kept track as best as I could of the people who came through our home for that year and lost count after 1,021. Many of the people we visited with there and especially the ones we have seen over here, claiming to have children diagnosed as LD, had children with nothing more than behavior problems. The parents could not control them. In many cases the parents were not *allowed* to control them. We are living in a day and age when parents are being told that it is unlawful for them to spank, remove phone privileges, restrict, or punish their own children. To do so could bring about the placement of your children in a foster care facility and you, as parents, in counseling or jail.

Yes, there are LD children. I more than anyone should know that. But, is it possible that this frenzy to label children as being LD could be another case of "The Emperor with No Clothes"?

Actually, does it really matter? The point is, these children can learn and will learn well when taught at home.

For those of you who really do have LD children consider the following:

• Let them learn at their own pace. If they love and excel in math, go for it. If they are still struggling to learn their alphabet at age ten, be patient.

• Focus in on the survival or home skills.

• Have them memorize Scripture.

I do not know why, but many LD children have an unusual ability to memorize and retain Scripture. In my daughter Emily's case, she couldn't remember her colors or numbers from one day to the next, but she had an amazing memory for Scripture. She has memorized whole Psalms and long chapters in Proverbs, Matthew, and

James, just to mention a few. Even as I write these words I know if I were to turn to her and ask her to quote James, chapter 1, she could do it with very few, if any, helps. Amazingly, she memorized James over four years ago.

One year while we were living in Colorado, the homeschooling laws changed. Part of the law stated that if homeschooled children ever fell below a certain percentage when tested, they could be ordered back into the public school system. I can still remember the chill of fear that swept through me when I read that provision, understanding full well the implications. That clause would not apply to Emily because of her educational handicap, yet I was still concerned. The next school year I pushed the academic side of her education and eased up on the Scripture memory, and at the end of the year her test scores dropped in almost every area. We got the message and resumed putting Scripture and the Lord first the next year and sure enough, her test scores improved dramatically.

This is just another reminder to teach your children, even those with LD, in the ways of the Lord, the fear of the Lord, and how to please Him.

College

While interviewing Inge Cannon, I was surprised to learn that this big push to get a college education came about after World War II. The G.I. bill was available and many men, without work, took advantage of it. Since then a college education has become even more affordable because of grants, scholarships, and loans, but is it the best option for your child?

To begin with, many colleges not only accept homeschooled children, they actively recruit them.

• At Oral Roberts University (ORU), your child can receive a four thousand dollar scholarship over four years just because they were homeschooled.

• Harvard, Yale, Princeton, Duke: all are big names as far as educational establishments go and all recruit homeschoolers.

• Colorado Christian University allows us to broadcast "Homeschooling Live" on the Home Education Radio Network from its campus in the foothills.

• ORU has designed what they call their College Preparatory Classes specifically for homeschoolers. Your son or daughter can take these classes by correspondence as young as age sixteen. If you should decide to go to another college, these classes are fully accredited and allow you to attend another university as a transfer student.

Homeschooled children have gained the reputation of being serious, capable students who have learned how to learn. *Homeschooling for Excellence* by David and Micki Colfax tells how they homeschooled their sons, all of whom were accepted into Harvard. Their eldest son appeared on "The Phil Donahue Show" as a result.

Let's not forget the Swan family, whose ten children typically graduated high school by age eleven, received their bachelor's degree by age fifteen and their master's by age sixteen. They used correspondence courses from Brigham Young University with no problems.

Another option to consider is apprenticeship. Apprenticeship may be the wave of the future, allowing young men and women the opportunity for one-on-one personal training and tutoring by godly mentors. Whatever your choice, remember to bring it before the Lord and seek His mind on it rather than do what everyone else does just as a matter of course.

Recommended Reading and Resources

1. Inge Cannon, *Education Plus* tapes and materials: 803-281-9316.

2. For information on Oral Roberts University Prepatory Classes, call at 1-800-678-8876.

3. Jerome Rosner, *Helping Children Overcome Learning Difficulties* (New York: Walker Publishing Co., 1975).

Checklist

___ STEP ONE: I am not only convinced to homeschool, but I am convicted by the Holy Spirit that this is God's will for my life.

___ STEP TWO: I have organized and consolidated all my incoming homeschooling material into one place.

___ STEP THREE: I have purchased or put together a notebook of some kind and have transferred all my notes, addresses, etc., into it.

___ STEP FOUR: I have secured a copy of my state laws and know fully what my legal right to homeschool is.

___ STEP FIVE: I have evaluated my learning style and that of my children and have a pretty good handle on how we assimilate information.

___ STEP SIX: I have reviewed the two main approaches to education and know which direction the Lord would have my family head.

___ STEP SEVEN: I understand the three basic types of curriculum available and am ready to start shopping for the one that meets the needs of my family.

___ STEP EIGHT: I have looked over the list of supplies required for my homeschooling program and have put together or purchased what I need.

___ STEP NINE: I have gone on a date with my husband and we have clearly defined our roles and responsibilities in our homeschool decision.

___ STEP TEN: I have sat down with my calendar and worked out a schedule for the yearly, as well as the daily, hours we want to homeschool.

___ STEP ELEVEN: I have made a list of all the chores and responsibilities within the home and have developed a plan to teach these skills.

___ STEP TWELVE: I have looked over the list of tools available to me within my area and plan to schedule them in or utilize them in my program.

___ STEP THIRTEEN: I have looked over the fast track section and have taken appropriate steps for my child (where appropriate).

___ STEP FOURTEEN: I have worked out a budget and feel I can create the things that I cannot purchase at this time.

___ STEP FIFTEEN: I have read the section on home industries and have some ideas about a future home industry for my family.

___ STEP SIXTEEN: I have read the information on ministry, colleges, and learning disabilities and know what areas apply to our family.

Step Seventeen:

Networking with HEN Radio

Terry and I met while in Mexico on a Missionary Apprenticeship Program, and so missions have always been near and dear to us. In 1982 while we were attending a missions conference, the Lord touched us with the knowledge that He wanted to use us around the world. We began to look for a country to serve in and thought long and hard about Iceland. The more we studied the country, the more we could picture ourselves there. That was a difficult time in our lives because Terry was in Bible college and all our friends seemed to know exactly what God had called them to do and where He was calling them to do it in. It seemed like God was holding back with us, which made us all the more impatient.

By this time, the full extent of Emily's medical situation was known and the mission boards we spoke with were reluctant to accept our family for service. Their attitude caused us to think long and hard about the "systems and traditions" we have built up over the past hundred years. How biblical are they? Around this time the Lord showed us 2 Chronicles 16:9, "For the eyes of the Lord search back and forth across the whole earth, looking for people whose hearts are perfect toward him, so that he can show his great power in helping them." We both sensed the Lord asking us, "Do you want to be those people?" More than anything, that is what we wanted, and that meant that God was going to lead us down a different path—one of faith—if we were willing.

God began to give us an unexplainable, unnatural affection for the people of New Zealand until the summer of 1988, when we put our businesses up for sale in order to serve Him there. The Lord put us on hold for another year, and then worked mightily to move us to New Zealand, the how and why of which is a whole other book. All we knew was that God wanted us in New Zealand to share Jesus with those who didn't have Him and to encourage the ones who did.

At that time, New Zealand was going through a difficult time economically, causing families who could no longer afford private, Christian education to look to homeschooling and to us. Soon so many families were coming that a church allowed the use of their facilities for a Saturday workshop. We worked hard to come up with a workbook of some sort that we could use to give them information and encouragement and presented it as best we could. As word spread and the need increased, we were being asked to present workshops all over the country. During this time we met many wonderful families totally sold out to the Lord and sacrificially dedicated to their children. We also saw an isolation among the homeschoolers and the difficulty they were having connecting and networking with one another. It was then that the concept of a Home Education Network was born. At that time we had the idea of providing some sort of a newsletter that would provide the connectivity that was needed. Although the homeschooling leadership of the country agreed with us in theory, there was difficulty in getting everyone together on the concept of a central publication. As we prepared to leave New Zealand, we formed a board of directors to carry on with the concept until we returned. The last week we were in the country, we were invited to be on a Sunday morning radio program for children. We discussed homeschooling and, at the last moment, the DJs opened the phone lines for questions. None of us could have anticipated the incredible response. Calls came in from all over the country, creating confusion and hilarity in the studio as lines became tangled and calls got mixed up.

This was it. This was the connecting rod God wanted to use to draw the homeschooling community together, but now we were leaving! Nevertheless, it planted a seed.

We came back to the States, planning to be here only six months and then to return; however, God had other plans.

While back in the States we gave some homeschooling workshops and were invited to be guests on a small local radio station in northern Colorado. The programs were so well received we spoke to the station owner about making it a regular feature. On 12 March 1994, the first one-hour broadcast of the Home Education Radio Network was aired.

The program and concept were very well received, and before too long we added another hour and went to prime time, Saturday morning 8:00 to 10:00 A.M. mountain standard time. In June we began distribution over a national satellite, and in October we were picked up by a short-wave station that went into eighty-four countries in Europe.

On 1 July 1995, we moved to the largest Christian radio station in Colorado, KWBI 91.1 FM, and began distribution on the largest Christian satellite provider in the world. Another short-wave provider has picked us up and is now sending us throughout the Pacific Rim, including New Zealand, via airwaves. We have finally returned to New Zealand!

"For the eyes of the Lord search back and forth across the whole earth, looking for people whose hearts are perfect toward him, so that he can show his great power in helping them" (2 Chron. 16:9).

Status

Currently the Home Education Radio Network (HEN Radio) produces a two-hour talk radio program called "Homeschooling Live" every Saturday morning from 11:00 A.M. to 1:00 P.M. mountain standard time. It is broadcast by three short-wave providers into Europe and the Pacific Rim. To date we have had letters and calls from

> Australia
> Canada
> Mexico
> New Zealand
> Papua New Guinea
> South Africa
> Sweden

As of September 1995, we are carried by forty other stations and translators, covering parts of

> Alaska
> California
> Colorado
> Hawaii
> Illinois
> Indiana
> New Mexico
> Ohio
> Oklahoma
> Tennessee
> Texas
> West Virginia
> Wisconsin
> Wyoming

Format

"Homeschooling Live" is a two-hour talk radio program addressing the needs of homeschoolers. The first hour I am able to interview nationally known guests such as Phyllis Schlafly, Ken Wales (producer of the "Christy" series), Michael Farris, Dr. Ruth Beechick, and others. Listeners are encouraged to call in with their questions and comments as well.

During the second hour, I present new books and curricula, usually interviewing the creators or authors. We have a fifteen-minute legislative update, during which contact with the Rutherford Institute, HSLDA, and others inform our listeners of any legal or legislative changes that could seriously impact homeschooling families.

Throughout the program we have ninety-second special segments presented by people and organizations such as Dinah Monahan, creator of the "Busy Women's Daily Planner," Jennifer Steward, creator of the *Choreganizer,* Martha Whitney of *Home Sweet Home* magazine, HSLDA, and the Rutherford Institute, to name a few.

Meet our Sponsors and Segment Providers

Sponsor: Colorado Christian University (CCU)

CCU is *the* Christian University of the Rocky Mountain region with a developing heart and vision for the homeschooler. KWBI, a radio ministry of CCU, is the radio home for HEN Radio located in the beautiful foothills of the Morrison campus. CCU recognizes the quality education of homeschooling and seeks to work with homeschoolers and their parents to assure that the same values, morals, and high academic standard established in the home will be carried out in the university. CCU offers over twenty-five undergraduate majors, three graduate programs, and continuing education for the adult learner. For more information and to thank CCU for their involvement with HEN Radio, you may contact the Admissions Office at 303-202-0100.

Sponsor: Great Christian Books (GCB)

GCB, founded twenty-five years ago, has been committed to providing the very best in written materials—whether books, Bibles, commentaries, or homeschooling curricula—at drastically discounted prices. Their heart is for committed Christians on a limited budget or those wanting to be careful with the resources God has given them. GCB carefully screens all materials submitted to them for distribution, assuring the reader that anything in their free catalog is of the highest quality. We have personally met the leadership of GCB and believe their heart for God, their passion for honesty and service, and their commitment to excellence have contributed to their being the largest discount Christian curriculum provider in the world. They are our "on the air" bookstore and carry nearly all of the products we present to our listeners. We are proud to have them as our founding sponsor. For a free catalog, you may call 800-775-5422. If you like what you hear on HEN Radio, thank GCB for helping to make it possible!

Sponsor: Homeschooling Today Magazine (HTM)

The homeschooling magazine market has literally exploded, with new ones emerging every other month. What makes *HTM* unique is that it is also a curriculum resource that you can actually teach from. Along with the articles and information designed to encourage you, *HTM* provides you with material each month in unit study form that you can use in your own homeschooling instruction. Their advertisers are very tastefully presented, providing the reader with enough information to allow them to make informed choices rather than impulse purchases. Subscriptions to *Homeschooling Today Magazine* are only sixteen dollars for one year (six issues), and for those of you who mention HEN Radio, a portion of your subscription goes directly to HEN Radio for its ministry. For more information or to order your subscription, you may call 305-963-1132 or write to *Homeschooling Today Magazine*, P.O. Box 5863 Department A, Hollywood, FL 33083.

Segment Provider: Dr. Brian Ray
National Home Education Research Institute

NHERI is a nonprofit research and educational organization. NHERI conducts and evaluates research to enhance the use of home and family in educating children. NHERI specializes in (a) producing quality research on home education, (b) serving as a clearinghouse of research for home educators, researchers, policy makers, and the media, and (c) educating the public concerning the findings of all such research. Dr. Brian Ray, NHERI's President, uses the weekly Research Report to bring alive an area of research which highlights the crucial nature of parents and the family in areas such as children's early education, physical health, academic achievement, socialization, and success in adulthood. Dr. Ray makes research understandable, engaging, and useful. For more information about NHERI, the journal *Home School Researcher*, and numerous other print, audio, and video publications, call 503-375-7019 or write to Dr. Brian Ray, NHERI, 5000 Deer Park Drive SE, Salem, OR 97301.

Segment Provider: Dinah Monahan
The Busy Woman's Daily Planner

Over thirteen years ago I began using a notebook, and through the years I have tried out every one ever produced until I discovered *The Busy Woman's Daily Planner* created by Dinah. This planner meets my needs as a Christian wife, mother, and now homeschooler because of the homeschooling planning sheets I was able to design exclusively for Dinah. The most remarkable thing about Dinah's planner is the combination notebook/purse that allows me to combine them into one. Dinah's gift for organization is reflected in the ninety second segment you hear each week exclusively on HEN Radio in which she gives tips to keep us organized and at our optimum production capacity. To receive Dinah's free *Organizational Tips* newsletter and to receive more information about her planner, call 800-858-3040. Please be sure to let her know how much you appreciate hearing her on HEN Radio.

Segment Provider: Michael Sharman
Victories in the Battle for America

In a day and age when we are continually bombarded with news designed to depress any optimist, we need a godly man like Mike Sharman. Each month Mike, a homeschooling father and an attorney, publishes a newsletter that reports the many encouraging victories that have taken place in the courts that you never hear about on the nightly news. Mike publishes accurate details of court victories that have held up traditional family values in cases that involve homeschooling, abortion, homosexuality, and our public schools to name a few. Each week Mike highlights one case to encourage you; however, you can enjoy six pages of victories every month and support HEN Radio by ordering a yearly subscription. For more information you may call 540-825-9600 or write to him at 114 N. West St., Culpepper, VA 22701.

Segment Provider: The Rutherford Institute
Freedom under Fire

The Rutherford Institute (TRI) is a nonprofit civil liberties organization specializing in the defense of religious liberty. TRI works in five priority areas: preserving free speech, protecting the right of church and religious groups to operate freely, defending family and parental autonomy, supporting the sanctity of human life, and defending human rights across the globe. Each week on "Freedom under Fire," John Whitehead, TRI's president, highlights cases and current events that pertain to your freedoms as a homeschooler and as a religious person. For more information about the Rutherford Institute, call Sarah Chamberlain at (804) 978-3888 or write to her at P.O. Box 7482, Charlottesville, VA 22906.

Segment Provider: Teri Spray
Curriculum Considerations

Teri and her husband, Mike, founded Christian Cottage Schools (CCS) in 1986. CCS is a national satellite school that uses diagnostic testing to create an individualized curriculum for each enrolled student. Teri personally selects or approves curriculum items from various publishers for each student and monitors all students' progress from year to year. Consequently, Teri is our resident expert on the pros and cons of almost any curriculum produced. Christian Cottage Schools is an option any homeschooler should consider because of the individualized care, support services, and nationally recognized graduation diploma. For more information about CCS and to thank Teri for her excellent curriculum reviews, you may call 303-369-1678 or write to her at 3560 W. Dawson Rd., Sedalia, CO 80135.

Segment Provider: Martha Whitney
Home Health Hints

Martha and her husband, Stuart, publish the terrific *Home Sweet Home* magazine. This is the magazine that I particularly enjoy for its back-to-basics and natural content. This magazine really helps the family look to the home for ideas about home industries, herbs and natural medicines, even home birth! Martha takes information from her magazine each week to give the homeschooler a ninety-second idea for taking care of our health needs in the home. To find out more about her magazine and tell her how much you appreciate her segment on HEN Radio you can write to *Home Sweet Home* magazine, Stuart and Martha Whitney, 2462 Lawrence Cove Rd., Eva, AL 35621.

Segment Provider: Karey Swan
The Heart of the Home

Karey is a homemaking consultant, Bosch Kitchen machine distributor, and regional representative for the KONOS character-unit study curriculum. She draws on all the experience she has from grinding her own grains, breadmaking, gardening, root-cellaring, canning, studying nutrition, and quilting to provide the homeschooler with a ninety-second homemaking nutrition tip each week. She has a concert and seminar ministry with her husband, Monte, and writes and speaks from her eighteen years of homeschooling experience. To find out more about Bosch kitchen machines, KONOS, and Karey's breadmaking classes and recipes, or to tell her how much you appreciate her part in HEN Radio, call 303-670-0673 or write Singing Springs Productions, P.O. Box 3883, Evergreen, CO 80439.

Segment Provider: Jennifer Steward
Winning the Chore Wars

Jennifer Steward, homeschooling mother of six, is the creator of the popular chore system, the *Choreganizer*. She and her husband, Jim, are the founders of their homeschooling mail order business, Steward Ship. Together they work hard to find positive ways to encourage and restore the much needed work ethic of days gone by, so children can become industrious, self-directed adults. To learn more about Jennifer's *Choreganizer* or to receive her free homeschooling catalog, call Steward Ship at 916-333-1642. To purchase a *Choreganizer* using your credit card call Noble Publishing Associates at 800-225-5259.

Segment Provider: Phyllis Schlafly
The Education Report

Constitutional attorney and creator of "The First Reader" reading system, Phyllis Schlafly keeps us informed about curricula in our public schools and legislation that affects all schools. Homeschoolers are greatly affected by the direction and agenda of the public schools and need to keep on their toes in order not to lose their right to homeschool through ungodly manipulation. To find out more about her "First Reader" system or how to get a copy of the *Education Report*, write Eagle Forum, Alton, IL 62002, or call 800-700-5228.

Segment Provider: Home School Legal Defense Association
Home School Heartbeat

Home School Heartbeat is provided by the Home School Legal Defense Association (HSLDA). HSLDA was founded in 1983 to bring together a large number of homeschooling families so that each can have a low cost method of obtaining quality legal defense. They give families the freedom to homeschool without fear of facing legal threats alone. They also work with state home-schooling organizations and legislators to get good homeschooling laws in place in every state in the union. For a free copy of your state homeschooling laws and application to have these attorneys on retainer for you, as they are for over forty-five thousand other homeschooling families, call 540-338-5600 or write P.O. Box 1835, Leesburg, VA 22075.

HEN Radio is a a nonprofit ministry supported entirely by the gifts and donations of individuals and businesses who believe in its mission. By not taking advertising dollars, we are free to expose and promote the best of the best in homeschooling.

Vision

You don't have to be a rocket scientist to figure out that the family is under a great deal of attack and is rapidly loosing its freedoms. Each week a new piece of legislation comes to light that threatens the family and, potentially, the right to homeschool.

Our vision is to facilitate homeschooling for every family throughout the world via radio waves and to become a weekly source of encouragement and information by a simple turn of the knob.

Furthermore, we feel called to be a "watchman on the wall," sounding the alarm when another attack is leveled against the family. The only way for HEN Radio to be effective in this vision is for homeschoolers all over the country to pull together to get the program on in their area.

The next few years will be a pivotal time in America's history, and I believe God wants to use homeschooling families to make a difference. It is not too late to stand for what God wants and be counted among the faithful, no matter what the cost or what it takes.

If you cannot tune in "Homeschooling Live" in your area, you may call or write to us at:

The Home Education RADIO Network
P.O. Box 3338
Idaho Springs, CO 80452
303-567-4092
E-Mail HEN Radio @
AOL.COM

HEN Radio is available to every radio station in the country; however, there must be enough listener interest and support to warrant your local station carrying it. By simply following the steps outlined below, you can bring HEN Radio into your community!

1. Select a station in your area whose programming would be compatible with our broadcast. This station can be commercial or noncommercial.

2. Meet with your local homeschooling support group or related church group and discuss the situation. Agree together to target one particular station initially.

3. Have someone meet with the station manager, showing him a copy of the enclosed promotional sheet. This gives him all the technical information he needs to air the program.

4. Begin a phone-calling campaign to the station requesting the program. The more calls, the better. Three or four calls are nice, but thirty or forty calls are great.

5. Encourage local listener sponsorship. Look for businesses in your community that support home education or family values and ask them to financially support the program locally, if on a commercial station, or solicit donations if it is on a noncommercial station.

6. Notify us when the station does decide to pull in the program, and we will add it to our list in case someone else in your broadcast area inquires.

Finally, we ask that you keep in mind that HEN Radio is a charitable ministry and would greatly appreciate any prayers and financial support you or your local support group can offer.

Step Eighteen:

Vicki's Recommendations

In the late eighties, I was being asked to speak at more and more churches and ladies' retreats on a variety of subjects, homeschooling not necessarily being one of them. I enjoyed those opportunities so much I began to feel guilty. The enemy tried hard to convince me that because I enjoyed it so much, I must be speaking in the flesh. I worried about this and nearly gave up speaking altogether. After time spent in the Word and with the Lord, I knew that speaking out for Him was what He had called me to do.

What was it about speaking to large groups of people that was so rewarding? It was being able to share with them what God had done in my life and in my family's lives and to watch them light up with encouragement and hope, knowing that if God did these things for me, then perhaps He would do the same for them. Isn't that what the Scriptures are all about—a written history, testimony, and declaration of what God has done for others and what He wants to do for us? Remember, I am just a plain, not so old mom. If He can use me, He can use anybody. As a matter of fact, the more useless and worthless the vessel, the more glory He receives when He polishes and displays it.

God is the one who gave me the ability to run my mouth for two hours without taking a breath. God is the one who has taken me through refining fires, one after another, and given me the testimony of His unshakable faithfulness. And, God is the one who gives me unspeakable joy when I see someone in tears because something I said met their need.

The Best of the Best

What good do our successes and failures do for others if we keep them to ourselves? For that reason, I have included this chapter on my personal favorites regarding books, curricula, and products that I have used, tested, or reviewed over the years. I have included here the unusual things that few people have heard about, as well as popular items that I believe you should be encouraged to look into. What I haven't included are products that are "just okay" but that may earn me brownie points with their authors if I include them. There are many other products out there not on my lists, but that may be because I simply haven't reviewed them yet. To get good information on much of the homeschooling materials and products available, you need to get the free catalog from Great Christian Books, which includes limited reviews or the *Big Book of Home Learning* four-volume set by Mary Pride. As Christians we should be looking for the good, not dwelling on the bad, and for that reason I am giving you a list of the things I really like and think you might like too, not a list of what is really awful. Using the Curriculum Evaluation Sheets I have provided will give you a tool to use to write down the opinions of friends and family that have used materials you are considering.

Bibles

The Serendipity Bible (Littleton, CO: Serendipity House, 1988). This is great as a curriculum and as a personal study Bible.

The Life Application Bible—The Living Bible Edition (Wheaton, Illinois: Tyndale House Publishers, Inc., 1988). I know about the whole debate concerning using King James only versus other texts. As Terry's Bible college professor once said, "If you want the kids to get the cookies, put them on the bottom shelf." Parents should be grounded enough in the Word to see problems with different interpretations and discuss them with their children.

Kid's Application Bible (Wheaton, Illinois: Tyndale House Publishers, 1994). This Bible keeps their attention and helps them apply God's Word to their lives.

The Picture Bible (Elgin, Illinois: David C. Cook Publishing Co., 1978). Even little guys who cannot read enjoy this Bible. This Bible finally sparked an interest in reading for one of my sons.

The Toddler Bible by V. Gilbert Beers (Wheaton, Illinois: Victor Books/Scripture Press, 1992). Having personally met and interviewed Gill, I understand why I enjoy his material so much.

The Toddler Home Learning Kit by V. Gilbert Beers (Wheaton, Illinois: Victor Books/Scripture Press, 1994). This kit includes the Toddler Bible and is the best program I have seen for toddlers, as well as elementary-aged children. Dr. Beers has done more to help families realize what a treasure toddlers are than anyone I know.

Frogs in Pharaoh's Bed and 49 Other Fun Devotions for Kids by Mary Rose Pearson (Wheaton, Illinois: Tyndale House Publishers, Inc., 1995). I haven't had to ask my son if he's had his devotions since he got this book. It has fun facts, games, and loads of practical application.

CIBS (Children's Inductive Bible Study). This program, created by Janice Southerland, teaches creative thinking skills and practical application for Bible study that transfers over to other disciplines. For more information, you can write to Janice Southerland, Know & Grow in 2 Timothy, Children's Inductive Bible Studies, P.O. Box 17360, Colorado Springs, Colorado 80935.

Reading Programs

Parents for years have been taken in by phonics and reading programs that promise the moon and end up taking you to the cleaners. I began a serious review of as many reading programs as possible, comparing them by

- Cost
- Effectiveness
- Parent friendliness
- Drudge or delight for the children
- Help with unanswered questions

In my opinion, these were the best of the ones I reviewed.

TATRAS (Teach America To Read And Spell) by Frank Rogers. Hands down, this is the first one I would put money out for. At the time of this printing, it cost under forty dollars yet has all the bells and whistles you need to teach your child how to read painlessly and effectively. For more information, write or call Frank Rogers, *Teach America to Read and Spell*, P.O. Box 44093, Tacoma, WA 98444, 206-531-0312.

Fast Track by Jeannie Eller. Jeannie made a claim that there wasn't anyone out there that she couldn't teach to read, so Oprah Winfrey took her up on her claim, presenting her with four illiterate adults whom she taught to read in twelve days. Her program is both fun and effective. For more information, write or call Jeannie Eller, *Fast Track*, P.O. Box 4944, Cave Creek, AZ 85331, 1-800-378-1046.

The Pathway Reading Series (LaGrange, Indiana: Pathway Publishers, 1976). *Pathway* is an old-order Amish curriculum that is very inexpensive with black and white pictures. I never had to worry about what they would be reading in these books, and the phonics foundation is very sound.

Mathematics

Clever Kiwi Preschool Math. Along with retired headmaster Jack McDonald, Di Ritchie, a good friend from New Zealand, created this preschool program and it's on my list not because of my friendship with Di, but because it is very good material. It consists of interactive video with workbooks, and it lays the best foundation for mathematics concepts I have seen. They are working on the next level for elementary ages. I can't wait.

To get more information on the *Clever Kiwi Preschool Math Program,* contact the Home Education Radio Network at P.O. Box 3338, Idaho Springs, CO 80452, or call 303-567-4092.

Horizons Math, Grades K-3 (Tempe, Arizona: Alpha Omega Publications, 1994). Grades K through 3 are complete and terrific. They take what Dr. Stan Hartzler would call the salad approach, mixing in a little of everything every day, making for great review.

Language

Simply Grammar. Karen and Dean have taken Charlotte Mason's materials and republished them in America. Any time you find anything of Charlotte Mason's, it is worth investing in. For more information, contact Charlotte Mason and Karen Andreola, *Simply Grammar*, Charlotte Mason Research and Supply Company, P.O. 172, Stanton, New Jersey 08885.

Progeny Press *Study Guides to Literature* by Michael Gilleland (Eau Claire, Wisconsin: Progeny Press). Now this is the way great literature should by taught and looked at!

History

United States HIStory by Bob Cosby. Bob's approach to history is that it should be HIS story, meaning how Jesus Christ and the gospel were involved. In a day when history is constantly being rewritten, this book stands out as a testament to what really happened. This book may be unsettling to some of you who have swallowed error about our country's past. For more information, contact Bob Cosby, *United States HIStory,* Temple Baptist College, 19th Judicial District, 2711 S. East Street, Indianapolis, Indiana.

Organization

The Busy Woman's Daily Planner. I cannot say enough good things about this planner. Especially check out the purse/notebook cover that combines the two. For years I carried them separately and sometimes would leave one or the other in a store—but not anymore. For more information, contact Dinah Monaham, *The Busy Woman's Daily Planner,* 919 S. Main Street, Snowflake, AZ 85937, 1-800-858-4009.

Kid's Biz Planner. This is a planner, organizer, and contract for children that was created by moms who really understood children. I call it "The No More Nagging Notebook" that breeds responsibility. For more information, contact Debbie Hope and Cheri Ellison, *Kid's Biz Planner,* 24843 Del Prado Suite 491, Dana Point, CA 92629, 1-800-SELF-ESTEEM (1-800-735-3378).

Choreganizer. This is a chore system that is fun to use and really works. I used to make up my own chore charts until I discovered this one. It's quality work! For more information, contact Jennifer Steward, *Choreganizer,* Steward Ship, P.O. Box 164, Garden Valley, California 95633, 916-333-1642.

Emilie's Household Hints by Emilie Barnes (Eugene, Oregon: Harvest House Publishers, 1984). Emilie has several books that will help even the most unorganized homemaker find success.

Dinner's in the Freezer by Jill Bond (Elkton, Maryland: GCB Publishing Division, 1995). Don't let the title fool you. This book is a gold mine and has a lot more in it than cooking tips.

KONOS Curriculum and Compass. Even if you are not using the KONOS curriculum, I recommend that you get a copy of the *Compass*. The KONOS manuals can be used as a total curriculum, a supplement to other curricula or for family projects. For more information, contact Jessica Hulcey and Carole Thaxton, KONOS, P.O. Box 1534, Richardson, Texas 75083, 214-669-8337.

General Knowledge

Facts Plus by Susan C. Anthony. This book is so good we have included it in our Homeschool Starter Pac. Everything Susan has created is on our must-have list. Her *Facts Plus Activity Book* accompanies this book or stands alone. For more information, contact Susan C. Anthony, *Facts Plus*, Instructional Resources Company, P.O. Box 111704, Anchorage, Alaska 99511-1704, 907-345-6689.

Why Does Popcorn Pop? by Susan C. Anthony. This creative book gets kids noses into the *World Book Encyclopedia*. Your only problem will be in getting them out! For more information, contact Susan C. Anthony, *Why Does Popcorn Pop?* Instructional Resources Company, P.O. Box 111704, Anchorage, Alaska 99511-1704, 907-345-6689.

Helps

The Right Choice by Christopher J. Klicka (Gresham, Oregon: Noble Publishing Associates, 1993). This is in our Homeschool Starter Pac and needs to be read by anyone considering homeschooling. If you have to choose only one book to get at this time, this should be it.

Government Nannies by Cathy Duffy (Gresham, Oregon: Noble Publishing Associates, 1995). Just reading the introduction in this book made me so angry I tossed the book at the windshield of the car I was riding in. You need to read this book to understand where the educational system we have came from in order to de-program and think about doing things differently.

Out of Control: Who's Watching Our Child Protection Agencies by Brenda Scott (Lafayette, Louisiana: Huntington House Publishers, 1994). This is one of the most difficult books you will ever read. It will tear your heart out and make you angry, but it will also arm you with information to help you protect your family.

America's God and Country, Encyclopedia of Quotations by William Federer (Coppell, Texas: FAME Publishing Inc., 1994). This book has Washington, D.C., buzzing because of the actual quotes by famous Americans and others. It's a reference book that needs to be in every home in America.

No More Lone Ranger Moms by Donna Partow (Minneapolis, Minnesota: Bethany House Publishers, 1995). A must-read book for homeschool support groups.

How to Home School by Gayle Graham (Melrose, Florida: Common Sense Press, 1992). This book is so good it caused me to reconsider writing my own. It will give you another perspective on homeschooling. I really liked her sample forms.

How to Really Love Your Child by Dr. Ross Campbell, M.D. (Wheaton, Illinois: Victor Books, 1992). This answers questions you didn't know you had.

Child Training

Hints on Child Training by H. Clay Trumbull (Eugene, Oregon: Great Expectations Book Company, 1995). It was originally published in 1890, but it meets the needs of today.

Beautiful Girlhood by Karen Andreola (Eugene, Oregon: Great Expectations Book Co., 1995). This delightful book lives up to its title. Just reading this book makes you feel feminine!

Family Togetherness

Family Celebrations by Ann Hibbard (Grand Rapids, Michigan: Baker Books, 1995). Ann's books for Christmas, Easter, and Thanksgiving build family memories to last a lifetime. The devotions have corresponding crafts that are easy and enjoyable.

Pleasure

I usually have four to six books that I am reading at the same time. Most of these books I am reading to review for the program, but I try to have something to read purely for pleasure. Here are some of my favorites.

A Voice in the Wind by Francine Rivers (Wheaton, Illinois: Tyndale House Publishers, Inc., 1993). This book and its two sequels top my list. This book was so good I kept trying to read it while on my four-mile power walk. It didn't work!

The Chatain's Guardian by Robin Hardy (Waco, Texas: Word Books, 1984). This book and its two sequels may be hard to find but certainly worth the search.

The House of Winslow Series

The Honorable Imposter by Gilbert Morris (Minneapolis, Minnesota: Bethany House Publishers, 1986). *The Honorable Imposter* begins the historical and entertaining

House of Winslow Series. I have not been disappointed by anything I have read by Gilbert.

The Zion Chronicles and Covenant Series

The Gates of Zion by Bodie Thoene (Minneapolis, Minnesota: Bethany House Publishers, 1986). I have a hard time being patient waiting for Brock and Bodie to come out with their sequels. These books, beginning with *The Gates of Zion,* revolve around World War II and help put the historical events surrounding Israel into perspective.

Catalogs, Magazines and Newsletters

Homeschooling magazines and newsletters are plentiful. Consider asking for subscriptions to magazines as gifts for special occasions.

Great Christian Books Catalog. This free catalog gives reviews on products to help you make wise choices before you spend your money. To top it off, they provide the books you are looking for at lower prices than any other place I've found. After getting to know Phil Hibbard, I understand why God is blessing this business. You can contact Great Christian Books at P.O. Box 8000, Elkton, Maryland 21922-8000, 1-800-775-5422.

Victory in the Battle for America. This newsletter, published monthly by Mike Sharman, an attorney just outside of Washington, D.C., reveals the many victorious court decisions made that we never hear about. It is the most positive, encouraging newsletter you will ever read. For more information, contact Michael Sharman, "Victory in the Battle for America," 114 N. West Street, Culpepper, Virginia 22701, 540-825-9600.

Home Sweet Home magazine. Home remedies, childbirth experiences, herbs—this one is my personal favorite because it deals with issues I personally enjoy. For more information, contact Stuart and Martha Whitney, *Home*

Sweet Home magazine, 2462 Lawrence Cove Road, Eva, Alabama 35621, 205-482-2801.

Homeschooling Today Magazine. This is a magazine and curriculum all in one! I like magazines like this one because they have so much in them I have to take several sittings to get through them. *Homeschooling Today Magazine*, P.O. Box 5863 Department A, Hollywood, Florida 33083, 305-963-1132.

Home School Times. This delightful magazine is very entertaining. My children especially enjoy Benny's Best Adventure Club. For more information, contact *Home School Times* magazine, P.O. Box 2807, Napa, California 94558-0280, 1-800-600-3633.

Potpourri

Patch the Pirate. We heard our first *Patch the Pirate* tape in 1983 and have gotten them ever since. These are non-offensive, character-building, quality tapes that every grandparent should know about for their grandchildren. For more information, contact Majesty Music, P.O. Box 6524, Greenville, South Carolina 29606, 803-242-6722.

What Research Says about Home Schooling by Dr. Brian Ray. This video answers questions about homeschooling in an authoritative, compelling way. It will give you confidence and assurance that you have made the right choice to homeschool. For more information, contact Dr. Brian Ray, *What Research Says about Home Schooling*, National Home Education Research Institute, Western Baptist College, 5000 Deer Park Drive, S.E. Salem, Oregon 97301, 503-375-7019.

An Introduction to Self Defense by Don Daly. A self-defense tape made by a gentle giant to give children an understanding and respect for self-defense techniques rather than a "kick 'em, hit 'em" pump session. For more information, contact Don Daly, *An Introduction to Self Defense*, 303-287-4208.

Pilgrim's Progress Game. This is sure to be the Christian Monopoly found in every home. Not only is it a well-produced game, it's really fun. For more information, contact the Pilgrim's Progress Game, Family Time Inc., P.O. Box 3833, Bozeman, Montana 59772, 406-583-7542.

The Master's Family Puzzle Series by Ron DiCianni (Elgin, Illinois: Chariot Family Publishing, 1995). Ron is the artist behind the covers of Perretti's *Darkness* books. His artwork is now on puzzles designed to stimulate family discussion and closeness. Even more beautiful than his paintings, however, is Ron's heart for God.

Teaching through Movies by Dr. Arnold Burron. Dr. Burron takes you through the film classic *Where the Red Fern Grows* and teaches you how to use your critical thinking skills. His understanding of scriptural truth and its practical application is refreshing. For more information, contact Dr. Arnold Burron, Teaching through Movies, Sopris West, 1140 Boston Avenue, Longmont, Colorado 80501, 303-651-2829.

Appendix A:

Homeschooling Organizations

Essential Addresses

The Rutherford Institute
P.O. Box 7482
Charlottesville, VA 22906-7482
(804) 978-3888

The Home School Legal Defense Association
P.O. Box 159
Paeonian Springs, VA 22129
(540) 338-5600

State Homeschooling Organizations

Alabama
Christian Home Education Fellowship of Alabama
P.O. Box 563
Alabaster, AL 35007
205-664-2232

Alaska
Alaska Private and Home Educators Association
P.O. Box 141764
Anchorage, AK 99514
907-753-3018

Arizona
Arizona Families for Home Education
P.O. Box 4661
Scottsdale, AZ 85261-4661
602-443-0612

Christian Home Educators of Arizona
P.O. Box 13445
Scottsdale, AZ 85267-3445

Northern Arizona Home Educators
P.O. Box 30082
Flagstaff, AZ 86003-0082

Arkansas
Arkansas Christian Home Education Association
P.O. Box 4410
North Little Rock, AR 72116
501-758-9099

California
Christian Home Educators Association
P.O. Box 2009
Norwalk, CA 90651
310-864-2432 or 800-564-CHEA

Family Protection Ministries
910 Sunrise Avenue Suite A-1
Roseville, CA 95661

Colorado
Christian Home Educators of Colorado
1015 South Gaylord Street #226
Denver, CO 80209
303-388-1888

Concerned Parents for Colorado
P.O. Box 547
Florissant, CO 80902

Connecticut
The Education Association of Christian Homeschoolers
25 Field Stone Run
Farmington, CT 06032

Delaware
Delaware Home Education Association
P.O. Box 1003
Dover, DE 19903
302-653-6878

Tri-State Home School Network,
P.O. Box 7193
Newark, DE 19714
302-234-0516

District of Columbia
Bolling Area Home Schoolers of D.C.
1516E Carswell Circle
Washington, D.C. 20336

Florida
Florida Parent-Educators Association
3781 S.W. 18th Street
Ft. Lauderdale, FL 33312
407-723-1714

Florida Coalition of Christian
    Private School Administrators
5813 Papaya Drive
Ft. Pierce, FL 34982
407-465-1685

Georgia
Georgia Home Education Association
245 Buckeye Lane
Fayetteville, GA 30214
770-461-3657

North Georgia Home Education Association
200 West Crest Road
Rossville, GA 30741

Georgia for Freedom in Education
209 Cobb Street
Palmetto, GA 30268
770-463-1563

Hawaii
Christian Homeschoolers of Hawaii
91-824 Oama Street
Ewa Beach, HI 96706
808-689-6398

Idaho
Idaho Home Educators
Box 4022
Boise, ID 83711
208-323-0230

Illinois
Illinois Christian Home Educators
Box 310
Mt. Prospect, IL 60056
847-670-7150

Christian Home Educators Coalition
Box 470322
Chicago, IL 60647
312-278-0673

Indiana
Indiana Association of Home Educators
408 S. 9th Street, Suite 203
Noblesville, IN 46060
317-770-0644

Iowa
Network of Iowa Christian Home Educators
Box 158
Dexter, IA 50070
515-830-1614 or 800-723-0438 (in Iowa)

Kansas
Christian Home Education Confederation of Kansas
P.O. Box 3564
Shawnee Mission, KS 66203
316-945-0810

Kentucky
Christian Home Educators of Kentucky
691 Howardstown Road
Hodgensville, KY 42748
502-358-9270

Kentucky Home Education Association
P.O. Box 81
Winchester, KY 40392-0081

Louisiana
Christian Home Educators Fellowship
P.O. Box 74292
Baton Rouge, LA 70874-4292
504-642-2059

Maine
Homeschoolers of Maine
H.C. 62 Box 24
Hope, ME 04847
207-763-4251

Maryland
Maryland Association of Christian
    Home Education Organizations
P.O. Box 21701
Frederick MD 21701
301-663-3999

Christian Home Educators Network
304 North Beechwood Avenue
Catonsville, MD 21228
410-744-8919

Massachusetts
Massachusetts Home Schooler's
    Organization of Parent Educators
15 Ohio Street
Wilmington, MA 01887
508-685-1061

Michigan
Information Network for Christian Homes
4934 Cannonsburg Road
Belmont, MI 48333
616-874-5656

Christian Home Educators of Michigan
P.O. Box 2357
Farmington Hills, MI 48333
810-626-8431

Minnesota
Minnesota Association of Christian Home Educators
P.O. Box 188
Anoka, MN 55303
612-717-9070

Mississippi
Mississippi Home Educators Association
109 Reagan Ranch Road
Laurel, MS 39440
601-649-6432

Missouri
Missouri Association of Teaching Christian Homes
307 E. Ash Street, #146
Columbia, MO 65201
314-443-8217

Families for Home Education
400 East High Point Lane
Colombia, MO 65203
816-826-9302

Montana
Montana Coalition of Home Schools
P.O. Box 43
Gallatin Gateway, MT 59730
406-587-6163

Nebraska
Nebraska Christian Home Educators Association
P.O. Box 57041
Lincoln, NE 68505-7041
402-423-4297

Nevada
Home Education and Righteous Training
P.O. Box 42262
Las Vegas, NV 89116

New Hampshire
Christian Home Educators Of New Hampshire
P.O. Box 961
Manchester, NH 03105

New Jersey
Education Network of Christian Homeschoolers
65 Middlesex Road, Matawan, NJ 07747
908-583-7128

New Mexico
New Mexico Christian Home Educators
5749 Paradise Blvd., NW
Albuquerque, NM 87114
505-897-1772

New York
Loving Education at Home
P.O. Box 88
Cato, NY 13033
716-346-0939

North Carolina
North Carolinians for Home Education
419 North Boylan Ave.
Raleigh, NC 27603
919-834-6243

North Dakota
North Dakota Home School Association
4007 North State Street
Route 5 Box 9
Bismark, ND 58501
701-223-4080

Ohio
Christian Home Educators of Ohio
P.O. Box 262
Colombus, OH 43216
614-474-3177

Home Education Action Counsel of Ohio
P.O. Box 24133
Huber Heights, OH 45424

Oklahoma
Christian Home Educators Fellowship of Oklahoma
P.O. Box 471363
Tulsa, OK 74147-1363
918-583-7323

Oklahoma Central Home Educators
P.O. Box 270601
Oklahoma City, OK 73137

Oregon
Oregon Christian Home Education Association Network
2515 NE 37th
Portland, OR 97212
503-288-1285

Pennsylvania
Christian Home School Association of Pennsylvania
P.O. Box 3603
York, PA 17402-0603
717-661-2428

Pennsylvania Home Schoolers
RD 2, Box 117
Kittanning, PA 16201
412-783-6512

Rhode Island
Rhode Island Guild of Home Teachers
P.O. Box 11
Hope, RI 02831-0011
401-821-1546

South Carolina
South Carolina Home Educators Association
P.O. Box 612
Lexington, SC 29071
803-951-8960

South Carolina Association of Independent
    Home Schoolers
P.O. Box 2104
Irmo, SC 29063
803-551-1003

South Dakota
Heart for South Dakota
HCR 74, Box 28
Murdo, SD 57559
605-869-2508

Tennessee
Tennessee Home Education Association
3677 Richbriar Court
Nashville, TN 37211
615-834-3529

Texas
Home-Oriented Private Education for Texas
P.O. Box 59876
Dallas TX, 75229-9876
214-358-2221

Texas Home School Coalition
P.O. Box 6982
Lubbock, TX 79493
806-797-4927

North Texas Home Education Network
Box 59627
Dallas TX 75229
214-234-2366

Family Education Alliance of South Texas
4719 Blanco Road
San Antonio, TX 78212
210-342-4674

South East Texas Home School Association
4950 F.M. 1960 W. Suite C3-87
Houston, TX 77069
713-370-8787

Utah
Utah Christian Homeschoolers
P.O. Box 3942
Salt Lake City, UT 84110-3942
801-255-4053

Vermont
Christian Home Education of Vermont
2 Webster Street
Barre, VT 05641
802-658-4561

Virginia
Home Educators Association of Virginia
P.O. Box 1810
Front Royal, VA 22630
703-635-9322

Washington
Washington Association of Teaching Christian Homes
N. 2904 Dora Road
Spokane, WA 99212

Washington Home School Organization
18130 Midvale Ave.
North Seattle, WA 98083

West Virginia
Christian Home Educators of West Virginia
P.O. Box 8770
South Charleston, WV 25303
304-776-4664

Wisconsin
Wisconsin Christian Home Educators
2307 Carmel Ave.
Racine, WI 53405
414-637-5127

Wyoming
Home Schoolers of Wyoming
221 West Spruce Street
Rawlins, WY 82301
307-324-5553

International Organizations

Canada
Alberta Home Educators Association
Box 3451
Leduc, Alberta, T9E 6M2:
403-986-4264

England
Education Otherwise
36 Kinross Road, Leamington Spa
Warks, ENGLAND, CV327EF
0926-886-826

Germany
Christian Home Educators on Foreign Soil
Mike and Diane Smith
1856 CSGP, PSC2 Box 8462, APO, AE 09012
06-372-4874

Japan
KANTO Home Educators Association
PSC 477, Box 45, FPO, AP 96306-1299

New Zealand
Christian Home Schoolers of New Zealand
4 Tawa Street, Palmerson North
New Zealand

Puerto Rico
Christian Home Educators of the Caribbean
Palmas Del Mar Mail Service
Box 888, Suite 273
Humacao, PR00791
809-852-5284

Appendix B:

Philosophy of Education

We believe home-educating facilitates and enhances family bonding and godly character development. It also promotes creativity and personal confidence while minimizing wrong peer pressures and peer dependencies. Socialization is not eliminated through home education but directed toward family members and selected other families. Home-educating is the way God has directed us to fulfill our God-given responsibility to train up our children. Our philosophy of home education is based on the following verses of Scripture, taken from the New International Version of the Bible.

Genesis 18:19: "For I have chosen him, so that he will direct his children and his household after him to keep the way of the LORD by doing what is right and just, so that the LORD will bring about for Abraham what he has promised him."

Deuteronomy 4:9: "Only be careful, and watch yourselves closely so that you do not forget the things your eyes have seen or let them slip from your heart as long as you live. Teach them to your children and to their children after them."

Deuteronomy 6:7: "Impress them on your children. Talk about them when you sit at home and when you walk along the road, when you lie down and when you get up."

Deuteronomy 11:19: "Teach them to your children, talking about them when you sit at home and when you walk along the road, when you lie down and when you get up."

Joshua 1:8: "Do not let this Book of the Law depart from your mouth; meditate on it day and night, so that you may be careful to do everything written in it. Then you will be prosperous and successful."

Psalms 78:3-4: "What we have heard and known, what our fathers have told us, we will not hide them from their children; we will tell the next generation the praiseworthy deeds of the LORD, his power, and the wonders he has done."

Psalms 127:

> Unless the LORD builds the house, its builders labor in vain. Unless the LORD watches over the city, the watchmen stand guard in vain. In vain you rise early and stay up late, toiling for food to eat, for he grants sleep to those he loves. Sons are a heritage from the LORD, children a reward from him. Like arrows in the hands of a warrior are sons born in one's youth. Blessed is the man whose quiver is full of them. They will not be put to shame when they contend with their enemies in the gate.

Psalms 128:

> Blessed are all who fear the LORD, who walk in his ways. You will eat the fruit of your labor; blessings and prosperity will be yours. Your wife will be like a fruitful vine within your house; your sons will be like olive shoots around your table.

> Thus is the man blessed who fears the LORD.
> May the LORD bless you from Zion all the days
> of your life; may you see the prosperity of Jerusa-
> lem, and may you live to see your children's chil-
> dren. Peace be upon Israel.

Proverbs 22:6: "Train a child in the way he should go, and when he is old he will not turn from it."

Malachi 4:6: "He will turn the hearts of the fathers to their children, and the hearts of the children to their fathers; or else I will come and strike the land with a curse."

Ephesians 6:4: "Father, do not exasperate your children; instead, bring them up in the training and instruction of the LORD."

Colossians 3:20: "Children, obey your parents in everything, for this pleases the LORD."

Colossians 3:21: "Fathers, do not embitter your children, or they will become discouraged."

1 Timothy 2:15: "But women will be saved through childbearing—if they continue in faith, love and holiness with propriety."

1 Timothy 3:4: "He must manage his own family well and see that his children obey him with proper respect."

1 Timothy 3:12: "A deacon must be the husband of but one wife and must manage his children and his household well."

2 Timothy 3:15: "And how from infancy you have known the Holy Scriptures, which are able to make you wise for salvation through faith in Christ Jesus."

Titus 2:4-5: "Then they can train the younger women to love their husbands and children, to be self-controlled and pure, to be busy at home, to be kind, and to be subject to their husbands, so that no one will malign the Word of God."

Daily Schedule

Time	Dad	Mom	Emily	Sam	Ben	James	Helen	Connie	Anna
6:00 AM									
6:30									
7:00									
7:30									
8:00									
8:30									
9:00									
9:30									
10:00									
10:30									
11:00									
11:30									
Noon									
12:30									
1:00									
1:30									
2:00									
2:30									
3:00									
3:30									
4:00									
4:30									
5:00									
5:30									
6:00									

Curriculum Evaluation Sheet

Curriculum	Learning Style Visual / Auditory / Kinesthetic			Grade Levels	User Friendly	Doctrine	Accessible	Graduation Certificate	Cost	Comments

Field Trip Record and Evaluation Sheet

Date Planned For:

	BEFORE		AFTER	
Destination		How much time did it take?		
Address		Were they Courteous?		
Telephone		Was it clean?		
Contact Person		Was it busy?		
Directions		Did it have rest rooms?		
Special Instructions		How much did it cost?		
Things to Bring		Would I recommend it?		
Travel Time Needed		Comments		

Planner

DATE:

Weekly Chore Chart

DATE: _____
FROM: _____
TO: _____

	Sunday	Monday	Tuesday	Wednesday	Thursday	Friday	Saturday
1							
2							
3							
4							
5							

Created by Home Education Radio Network

Weekly Educational Activity Planner

DATE:
FROM:
TO:

Children	Sunday	Monday	Tuesday	Wednesday	Thursday	Friday	Saturday
1							
2							
3							
4							
5							

We welcome comments from our readers. Feel free to write to us at the following address:

Editorial Department
Vital Issues Press
P.O. Box 53788
Lafayette, LA 70505

More Good Books from Vital Issues Press

Anyone Can Homeschool
How to Find What Works for You
by Terry Dorian, Ph.D., and Zan Peters Tyler

Honest, practical, and inspirational, *Anyone Can Homeschool* assesses the latest in homeschool curricula and confirms that there are social as well as spiritual and academic advantages to home education. Both veteran and novice homeschoolers will gain insight and up-to-date information from this important new book.

ISBN 1-56384-095-2

How to Homeschool (Yes, You!)
SALT SERIES BOOKLET
by Julia Toto

Relax, you're not alone. More and more Americans from every walk of life are opting for home education. *How to Homeschool (Yes, You!)* answers the questions most asked about home education: What's the best curriculum for my children? Is is legal? Are certified teachers better instructors than parents? What do I tell my mother-in-law?

ISBN 1-56384-059-6

Dinosaurs and the Bible
by David W. Unfred

Author David Unfred educates and entertains in his delightfully unique style, unlocking some of the ancient mysteries about these lumbering giants, the dinosaurs. Colorfully and thoroughly illustrated, the informative discussion on the origin and history of the dinosaurs and how they fit into the biblical understanding of history makes this book an excellent resource for home educational programs and elementary and middle-school classrooms. *Dinosaurs and the Bible* will take you on an adventure of discovery from creation to modern expeditions in search of living dinosaurs.

ISBN 0-910311-70-6

To Grow By Storybook Readers
(Phonics in Action)
by Janet Friend

The quality of education in America is a major concern, and many parents are turning to homeschooling to teach their children to read. The *To Grow By Storybook Readers* can greatly enhance any homeschooling reading program with gentle Christian instruction. The set consists of eighteen softbound Storybook Readers plus two Activity Books. The *To Grow By Storybook Readers* are designed to be used in conjunction with Marie LeDoux's PLAY'N TALK™ phonics program but will work well with any orderly phonics program.

Complete Set ISBN 0-910311-69-2

In His Majesty's Service:
Christians in Politics
by Robert A. Peterson

In His Majesty's Service is more than a book about politics. It's a look at how real men have worked out their Christian beliefs in the rough-and-tumble world of high-level government, war, and nation-building. From these fascinating portraits of great Western leaders of the past, we can discover how to deal with some of the most pressing problems we face today. This exciting, but historically accurate, volume is as entertaining as it is enlightening.

ISBN 1-56384-100-2

Out of Control—
Who's Watching Our Child
Protection Agencies?
by Brenda Scott

This book of horror stories is true. The deplorable and unauthorized might of Child Protection Services is capable of reaching into and destroying any home in America. No matter how innocent and happy your family may be, you are one accusation away from disaster. Social workers are allowed to violate constitutional rights and often become judge, jury, and executioner. Innocent parents may appear on computer registers and be branded "child abuser" for life. Every year, it is estimated that over 1 million people are falsely accused of child abuse in this country. You could be next, says author and speaker Brenda Scott.

ISBN 1-56384-080-4

Conquering the Culture
The Fight for Our Children's Souls
by David Paul Eich

Remember Uncle Screwtape? He was the charming C.S. Lewis character who tried to educate his nephew, Wormwood, on the art of destroying souls. Now, from a fictional town in Montana, comes a similar allegory. A parents' association hires two consultants to give advice on how to raise children. The dialogue that ensues between these consultants and the towns-people accurately reflects the culture war fragmenting America today. This compelling book is a valuable source of support for parents who need both answers and courage to raise moral children in an immoral world.

ISBN 1-56384-101-0

The Culture War in America:
A Society in Chaos
by Bob Rosio

Without the strong moral foundation of the Judeo-Christian tradition to sustain us, America is fragmenting into a variety of pagan sects. Radical feminism, earth worship, occult activity, and out-and-out hedonism are just a few of the belief systems driving our social policy. Today, we are at the cross-roads, but *The Culture War in America* shows how we can individually and collectively return America to the Christian values on which it was founded.

ISBN 1-56384-097-9

Outcome-Based Education: The State's Assault on Our Children's Values

by Peg Luksik/Pamela Hobbs Hoffecker

From health to the environment, from the enforcement of tolerance to the eradication of absolutes, Goals 2000 enjoins a vast array of bureaucratic entities under the seemingly innocuous umbrella of education. Unfortunately, traditional education is nowhere to be found in this strings-attached program concerned not with real learning, but with the indoctrination of politically correct thought and behavior. This articulate and thoroughly documented work reveals the tactics of those in the modern educational system who are attempting to police the thoughts of our children.

ISBN 1-56384-025-1

Getting Out: An Escape Manual for Abused Women

by Kathy L. Cawthon

Four million women are physically assaulted by their husbands, ex-husbands, and boyfriends each year. Of these millions of women, nearly 4,000 die. Kathy Cawthon, herself a former victim of abuse, uses her own experience and the expertise of law enforcement personnel to guide the reader through the process of escaping an abusive relationship. *Getting Out* also shows readers how they can become whole and healthy individuals instead of victims, giving them hope for a better life in the future.

ISBN: 1-56384-093-6

Handouts and Pickpockets:
Our Government Gone Berserk
by William P. Hoar

William P. Hoar, a noted political analyst, echoes the sentiments of millions of Americans who are tired of being victimized by their own government. Hoar documents attacks on tradition in areas as diverse as the family and the military and exposes wasteful and oppressive tax programs. This chronicle of our government's pitiful decline into an overgrown Nanny State is shocking, but more shocking is Hoar's finding that this degeneration was no accident.

ISBN 1-56384-102-9

Do Angels Really Exist?
Separating Fact from Fantasy
by Dr. David O. Dykes

Have you ever seen an angel? Don't be too quick to answer "no." For most of us, angels evoke images of winged, white figures frolicking from one cloud to another. But, according to the Bible, angels are God's armored warriors ready to protect His kingdom in heaven, as well as His beloved followers on earth. By citing dozens of fascinating angel encounters, the author presents evidence that angels roam the earth today, protecting and comforting God's people. You might be encountering angels without even knowing it.

ISBN 1-56384-105-3

Health Begins in Him:
Biblical Steps to Optimal
Health and Nutrition
by Terry Dorian, Ph.D.

This book is offered as a resource for all those who are hungry for knowledge about how to change their lives in ways that will enable them to preserve or maintain optimal health. The Bible is rich with exhortations about healthy living, and here the author introduces readers to a system that strengthens and nourishes the body while upholding a spiritual cure for the heart, soul, and mind. The Bible's clear, concise, and lively dialogue enhances this directory on foods, food preparation, life-style changes, and suggestions for renewal.

ISBN 1-56384-081-2

Children No More:
How We Lost a Generation
by Brenda Scott

Child abuse, school yard crime, gang-land murders, popular lyrics laced with death motifs, twisted couplings posing as love on MTV and daytime soap operas (both accessible by latch-key children), loving parents portrayed as the enemy, condom pushers, drug apologists, philandering leaders . . . is it any wonder that Christian values and role models are passé? The author grieves the loss of a generation but savors a hope that the next can be saved.

ISBN 1-56384-083-9

ALSO AVAILABLE FROM VITAL ISSUES PRESS

M8174-TN

10